Jeremy Taylor
The Awful English Grammar
Die schreckliche englische Grammatik

AF197695

Einfach und ohne dicke Grammatikschinken …

Wer kennt sie nicht, die Fallstricke der englischen
Sprache? Man denkt, es klappt schon ganz gut, und
dann weiß man doch wieder nicht, ob man sich mit *of,
by* oder *from* für die richtige Präposition entschieden
hat oder wie es um die Zeitenfolge bei *if*-Sätzen im
Konditional II bestellt ist. Jeremy Taylor besitzt lang-
jährige Erfahrung als Englischlehrer und kennt sich
mit den Problemen im Sprachunterricht aus. Er weiß:
Grammatik muss verstanden werden, und sein Buch
ist Beweis dafür, dass das sogar amüsant sein kann!
In leicht verständlichen Dialogen werden dem Leser
Mustersätze wie auf einem Tee-Tablett serviert und
am jeweiligen Kapitelende in einer Tabelle zusam-
mengefasst.

Jeremy Taylor lebt in Tschechien und ist Autor,
Englischlehrer und Fotograf. Seine Sammlungen
englischer Witze sind in fünfzig Sprachen erschienen,
bei dtv zweisprachig ‹English Jokes. Englische Witze›
(9484).

Jutta Bachmann, Anglistin und Romanistin sowie
promovierte Molekularbiologin, lebt in Norwegen.
Neben zahlreichen eigenen Veröffentlichungen coacht
und berät sie v. a. Wissenschaftler bei Sprachfragen
und Übersetzungen.

Jeremy Taylor

The Awful English Grammar

Die schreckliche englische Grammatik

Sieben amüsante Dialoge

Übersetzt von
Jutta Bachmann

Illustrationen von
Sabine Wilharm

dtv

Originalausgabe 2018
5. Auflage 2026
dtv Verlagsgesellschaft mbH & Co. KG
Tumblingerstraße 21, 80337 München
produktsicherheit@dtv.de

Umschlaggestaltung: dtv unter Verwendung
einer Illustration von Sabine Wilharm
Satz: Greiner & Reichel, Köln
Druck und Bindung: Druckerei C.H.Beck, Nördlingen
Printed in Germany · ISBN 978-3-423-09540-2

The Awful
English Grammar

Die schreckliche
englische Grammatik

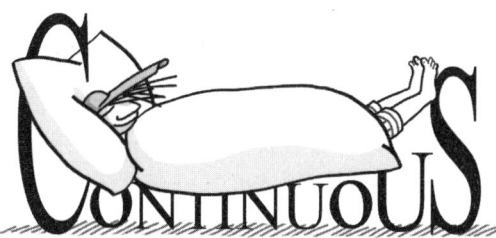

Inhalt

Introduction

SULLY

Meet Barry Buggins, an enthusiastic, but not particularly talented, man from England. At school Barry's favourite subject was wood-work but his teacher's report stated that the result of Barry's work was a time-consuming way of producing firewood. Barry spent three years racking up some serious debt as a student of archaeology and since then has had two jobs. The first job, shelf stacker at Pound-land, Barry managed to hold onto for over a month. The second, collecting and washing glasses in the King's Head, lasted just under three weeks.

Barry's family are keenly aware of the mis-match between Barry's enthusiasm and Barry's talent. They realise that a well-paid job in archaeology is not likely to jump into Barry's arms and that without some guidance, Barry could well spend his life drifting along from one

Zur Einführung

BARRY

Darf ich vorstellen: Barry Buggins, ein leidenschaftlicher, wenn auch nicht besonders begabter Mann aus England. In der Schule war sein Lieblingsfach das Arbeiten mit Holz. Aber im Zeugnis stand, dass sein Schaffen im Ergebnis eher eine zeitraubende Art und Weise war, Brennholz herzustellen. Als Archäologiestudent hat Barry dann drei Jahre lang beträchtliche Schulden angehäuft und in der Folge zwei Gelegenheitsjobs angenommen. Zuerst füllte er Regale bei Poundland auf; aber das hielt er gerade mal etwas über einen Monat aus. In seinem zweiten Job im King's Head Pub musste er Gläser einsammeln und in die Spülmaschine stellen. Diesen Job behielt er knapp drei Wochen.

Barrys Familie ist die Diskrepanz zwischen seiner Begeisterungsfähigkeit und seiner Begabung mehr als klar. Sie weiß auch, dass eine gut bezahlte Stelle in der Archäologie ihm nicht gerade zufliegen wird und dass er sich ohne Unterstützung wahrscheinlich von einem schlecht bezahlten Job zum

zero-hour contract job to another. This is where Aunt Rosemary comes into the picture.

Aunt Rosemary worked as an editor for a well-known publisher for twenty-six years and is now a lady of leisure. She saw the danger of her nephew, Barry, making a pig's ear of his working life, so found a TEFL course (Teaching English as a Foreign Language) where he could be converted from a failed shelf stacker and glass washer into a Professional English Teacher in just a month.

Three days after the course started, Rosemary got an email from one of the course directors. She, the course director, explained that despite being a native speaker and despite Barry being very enthusiastic, he didn't seem to be able to grasp some of the basic aspects of English grammar. This could possibly damage his chances of completing the course and would almost certainly

AUNT ROSEMARY

anderen hangeln wird. Wäre da nicht Tante Rosemary.

Tante Rosemary hatte sechsundzwanzig Jahre lang
als Lektorin in einem bekannten Verlag gearbeitet und
genoss nun ihren Ruhestand. Sie sah sehr wohl das Ri-
siko, dass ihr Neffe Barry womöglich nichts aus seinem
Leben machen würde. Sie wählte daher für Barry einen
TEFL-Kurs (Unterrichten von Englisch als Fremdsprache), der dazu beitragen sollte, innerhalb eines Monats
aus dem gescheiterten Regalauffüller und Gläserspüler
Barry einen qualifizierten Englischlehrer zu machen.

Drei Tage nach Kursbeginn bekam Rosemary eine
E-Mail von einer der Kursleiterinnen. Diese erklärte,
dass Barry, obwohl er Muttersprachler und sehr enthu-
siastisch sei, kaum die Grundlagen der englischen
Grammatik begreifen würde. Dies würde Barrys Chan-
cen, den Kurs erfolgreich abzuschließen, mindern, und
damit mit ziemlicher Sicherheit auch seine Aussichten

hinder his chances of getting a job as a Professional English Teacher that Barry was now so keen to be.

A few phone calls later, Rosemary managed to find a teacher trainer, Mr Sully, who was willing, for a rather large fee, to coach Barry. A series of seven sessions would easily be enough to allow Barry to get to grips with the complexities of English grammar and allow him to pursue his chosen career and to travel to Germany to be a Professional English Teacher. At least that is what the trainer thought before meeting Barry.

So what exactly happened when Barry met Sully? This is their story.

auf die gewünschte Arbeitsstelle als Englischlehrer zunichte machen.

Tante Rosemary führte ein paar Telefonate, und es gelang ihr, Mr Sully aufzutreiben. Sully bildete Englischlehrer aus und war gegen eine nicht unbeachtliche Summe bereit, Barry zu helfen. Sieben Unterrichtseinheiten sollten ausreichen, damit Barry die Vielschichtigkeit der englischen Grammatik in den Griff bekomme. So könnte er doch noch Englischlehrer werden und nach Deutschland reisen. Das war auf jeden Fall Mr Sullys Hoffnung, bis er Barry kennenlernte.

Wie also erging es Barry und Mr Sully?
Hier ihre Geschichte.

Futurity Or Futility?

"Okay now, Barry, we're going to start by looking at something pretty important in your life right now."

"Pot noodles?"

"No, not pot noodles. We're going to look at the future. You should know that English is an unusual language in that it has no future tense."

"You're pulling my leg!"

"No, really. English hasn't got a standardized future tense. Instead we use a dazzling array of auxiliary verbs and other tense forms which, by some miracle, speakers of English know that the speaker is referring to the future."

"Hold on, auxiliary verbs? What are they again?"

"Words like 'will', 'have' or 'can' which help the main verb. Some of them can also be full

Zukünftigkeit oder Nichtigkeit?

«Nun, Barry, werfen wir mal einen Blick auf etwas, das in deinem Leben gerade eine ziemlich große Rolle spielt.»

«Eine 5-Minuten-Terrine.»

«Nein, keine 5-Minuten-Terrine. Das Futur. Du musst nämlich wissen, dass die englische Sprache etwas ungewöhnlich ist. Hier gibt es nämlich kein Futur.»

«Willst du mir einen Bären aufbinden?»

«Nicht unbedingt. Aber die englische Sprache hat mehr als nur eine Möglichkeit, etwas in der Zukunft Liegendes auszudrücken. Wir benutzen eine beeindruckende Palette an Hilfsverben und andere Zeitformen, die Muttersprachler aber erstaunlicherweise als Futur erkennen.»

«Wart mal. Was sind jetzt gleich nochmal Hilfsverben?»

«Das sind im Englischen Wörter wie ‹will›, ‹have› oder ‹can›, wenn man sie zusammen mit einem Vollverb ver-

verbs, for example when I say 'I have a great bicycle'."

"I remember now. So, you mentioned 'a dazzling array' of forms. How many are there exactly?"

"Exactly? Gosh, I don't know."

"You don't know? And you call yourself an English teacher?"

"Well, there are four main ones and a few others which are less common. Let's make a start with the more common ones, shall we?"

"Ready when you are!"

"Well the most common way of expressing the future is simply by adding the auxiliary verb 'will' before a base verb form."

"Base verb form …"

"Yes, go, play, study … Have you got any plans for tonight?"

"Me? Tonight? No way. I'll be here until ten o'clock!"

"Excellent!"

"No it's not. I …"

"Your example was excellent. You made a simple *statement* about something in the future."

"You mean like one of those fortune tellers who look into a crystal ball and tell you 'You *will meet* a tall dark stranger who *will want* his wicked way with you'?"

wendet. Stehen sie für sich, sind sie selbst Vollverben, wenn ich zum Beispiel sage: ‹Ich habe ein tolles Fahrrad.›»

«Stimmt. Ich erinnere mich wieder. Du hast gesagt, dass es im Englischen eine beeindruckende Palette an Möglichkeiten gibt, das Futur auszudrücken. Wie viele genau?»

«Genau? Tja, das weiß ich leider nicht.»

«Du weißt das nicht? Und du willst Englischlehrer sein?»

«Nun, es gibt vier, die relativ oft verwendet werden, und dann noch ein paar, die weniger oft verwendet werden. Sollen wir mit den am häufigsten verwendeten anfangen?»

«Gerne. Also los!»

«Nun, die Verwendung des Hilfsverbs ‹will› in Kombination mit der Infinitivform eines Vollverbs ist wohl die häufigste Art und Weise, Zukunft auszudrücken.»

«Infinitiv …»

«Ja, gehen, spielen, studieren … Hast du heute Abend schon etwas vor?»

«Ich? Heute Abend? Keine Chance. Ich werde hier wohl nicht vor zehn rauskommen!»

«Prima!»

«Überhaupt nicht. Ich …»

«Ich habe dein Beispiel gemeint. Das war prima. Du hast eine einfache Aussage über ein Ereignis in der Zukunft gemacht.»

«Du meinst so wie eine Wahrsagerin, die in eine Kristallkugel schaut und dann sagt: ‹Sie werden heute Abend einen großen dunklen Fremden treffen, und dieser führt nichts Gutes im Schilde›?»

"Exactly. The fortune teller has no control over your future. She is simply talking about events in the future. But when we are *making statements about the future* is not the only time we use the simple future or *will future.*"

"Where else would it be used?"

"We also use it when we make a *spontaneous decision.*"

"A *spontaneous decision*? Er, could you give me an example?"

"Sure, you're in your local restaurant and you've ordered your favourite meal …"

"Pot noodle!"

"Well, the waiter comes back to you and says, 'Terribly sorry, Mr Buggins, the pot noodle is off'. You reply …"

"In that case, *I'll have* some pop tarts instead!"

"Brilliant! A *spontaneous decision*! Another interesting point, your 'will' was contracted."

"It was?"

"Yes – you didn't say '*I will have* …' You said, '*I'll have* …'"

"But I would always use the contracted form!"

"So would ninety-nine per cent of the population. In fact it can sound aggressive if you tell a waiter 'I *will have* some pop tarts'. Some people feel that you shouldn't use contracted forms when you're writing in English but lots of people do."

«Ja genau. Die Wahrsagerin hat aber keine Kontrolle über deine Zukunft. Sie berichtet einfach nur über etwas, das in der Zukunft liegt. Aber dies ist nicht der einzige Fall, bei dem wir Engländer das Simple Future oder Will-Future nehmen.»

«Wo wird es sonst noch verwendet?»

«Wir verwenden es auch, um eine spontane Entscheidung auszudrücken.»

«Eine spontane Entscheidung? Kannst du mir hierfür ein Beispiel geben?»

«Klar doch. Stell dir vor, du bist in einem Restaurant und hast deine Lieblingsspeise bestellt.»

«Eine 5-Minuten-Terrine!»

«Nun, der Kellner kommt an deinen Tisch zurück und sagt: ‹Es tut mir furchtbar leid, Mr Buggins, wir haben keine 5-Minuten-Terrine mehr›, und du erwiderst ...»

«Dann nehme ich eben ein paar Pop-Tarts!»

«Klasse! Das war eine spontane Entscheidung! Und was auch noch wichtig ist, du hast ‹I› und ‹will› zusammengezogen.»

«Hab ich das?»

«Ja. Du hast nicht ‹I will have ...› gesagt, sondern ‹I'll have ...›»

«Aber das würde ich immer so machen!»

«So machen es wahrscheinlich neunundneunzig Prozent aller Leute. Würdest du zu einer Bedienung ‹I will have some pop tarts› sagen, dann klingt das zudem etwas offensiv. Manche Leute finden, dass man in der Schriftsprache keine zusammengezogenen Formen verwenden sollte, aber viele Menschen tun es trotzdem.»

"Okay, I've got it so far: I use *will future* when I'm *talking about events in the future over which I have no control.* I also use *will future* when I make a *spontaneous decision,* like when I have to change my order in a restaurant."

"Perfect! Now things start to get interesting."

"Do you mean interesting or difficult?"

"Just interesting to an intellectual like yourself."

"Gosh, thanks."

"Okay, now do you remember that guy who cheated you out of £ 100 in that poker game last week?"

"That little guy with red hair and a funny chin?"

"That's the one. What do you *intend* to do if you see him again?"

"I'm *gonna kick* his head in!"

"Could you say that a little more clearly?"

"I'm *going to kick* his head in!"

"Great!"

"I thought you didn't approve of violence."

"I said 'great' because of your excellent example! You told me of your *intention.* What you are *going to do* when you see the little guy with the red hair and the funny chin."

"Aha! So that's another way of talking about

«Okay. Ich habe verstanden. Ich verwende Simple Future, wenn ich über etwas spreche, das in der Zukunft liegt und über das ich keine Kontrolle habe. Und ich nehme Simple Future auch, um eine spontane Entscheidung auszudrücken, etwa, wenn ich in einem Restaurant meine Essensbestellung ändern muss.»

«Ganz genau! Aber nun wird es erst richtig interessant.»

«Meinst du interessant, oder meinst du schwierig?»

«Interessant. Auf jeden Fall für so Schlauköpfe wie dich.»

«Glück gehabt! Danke.»

«Na gut. Erinnerst du dich noch an den Typen, der dich letzte Woche beim Poker um hundert Pfund erleichtert hat?»

«Der Kleine mit den roten Haaren und dem witzigen Kinn?»

«Ja, genau der. Was wirst du machen, wenn er dir nochmal über den Weg läuft?»

«Ihm den Schädel einschlagen!»

«Könntest du das noch anders sagen?»

«Ich werde ihm den Schädel einschlagen.»

«Großartig!»

«Ich dachte, du hättest etwas gegen Gewalt?»

«Ich habe ‹großartig› gesagt, weil du ein sehr gutes Beispiel genannt hast! Du hast mir von deiner Absicht erzählt. Was du tun wirst, wenn du den Kleinen mit den roten Haaren und dem witzigen Kinn wiedersiehst.»

«Ach so! Dann kann man so auch ein Ereignis in der

the future, using *'going to'* when I tell you what I *intend to do*!"

"That's right!"

"I'm *going to work* as a teacher in Germany."

"Correct. Well, at least that is your *plan* or *intention*."

"I'm *going to be* a brilliant teacher like you."

"Thank you for the compliment. Now there's another time when we use *'going to'* to talk about events in the future."

"There is?"

"There certainly is. Do you know your colleague called Wayne?"

"Wayne? The guy's a complete airhead. He never comes to lectures. He hasn't done any extra reading. He spends about five minutes planning his lessons and they're all crap anyway ... And another thing, how do you know Wayne? And how did you know about my poker partners?"

"Your Aunt Rosemary is a very well connected woman. Okay, do you think Wayne's going to get his certificate?"

"No way! *He's going to fail* the course!"

"On what *evidence* do you base your damning judgement?"

"On the fact that he is a lazy airhead who never does any work!"

"So, you are looking at some kind of *evidence* about Wayne's future."

"Oh, I get you. This is another future form.

Zukunft ausdrücken? Ich verwende ‹going to›, wenn ich dir erzähle, was ich zu tun beabsichtige. »

« Genau ! »

« Ich werde als Lehrer in Deutschland arbeiten. »

« Richtig. Das ist auf jeden Fall dein Plan oder deine Absicht. »

« Ich werde so ein guter Lehrer sein wie du. »

« Danke für das Kompliment. Aber es gibt noch eine weitere Situation, in der wir das Going-to-Future verwenden, um über Ereignisse in der Zukunft zu sprechen. »

« Noch eine? »

« Klar doch ! Kennst du einen Kollegen von dir namens Wayne? »

« Wayne? Dieser Typ ist ein kompletter Schwachkopf. Der kommt nie zu Vorlesungen. Und macht auch nicht mehr, als er muss. Er braucht gerade mal fünf Minuten, um seine Unterrichtsstunden zu planen, und die sind alles andere als gut. Aber etwas anderes, woher kennst du Wayne? Und woher weißt du von meiner Pokerrunde? »

« Deine Tante Rosemary hat einen recht großen Bekanntenkreis. Also, glaubst du, dass Wayne es schaffen wird und sein Zeugnis bekommt? »

« Niemals ! Er wird durchfallen ! »

« Worauf begründest du dein niederschmetterndes Urteil? »

« Auf die Tatsache, dass er ein fauler Schwachkopf ist, der niemals seine Arbeit macht. »

« Da denkst du wohl an eine Art logische Folge in Hinblick auf Waynes Zukunft, oder? »

« Oh, verstehe. Das ist auch eine Zukunftsform. Wenn

When there is *evidence* of something *'going to happen'* then we use the *'going to'* future."

"That's right. Look outside. What can you see?"

"Big black clouds!"

"In which direction are those clouds headed?"

"They're heading in this direction – towards us."

"How convenient. So, we have our *evidence*. What do you think *is going to happen*?"

"It's *going to rain*!"

"Really? How do you know that?"

"Because of the black clouds!"

"Our evidence."

"Right! Okay, let me get this straight before we go on. In fact, I'll produce a little table and you can tell me what you think of it."

man etwas kommen sieht, dann nimmt man auch das Going-to-Future.»

«Genau. Schau einmal nach draußen. Was siehst du?»

«Dicke schwarze Wolken.»

«In welche Richtung ziehen diese Wolken?»

«Hierher – geradewegs auf uns zu.»

«Wie passend. Das ist also ein Anzeichen dafür, dass etwas passieren wird. Was, glaubst du, wird demnächst passieren?»

«Es wird regnen.»

«Wirklich? Woher willst du das wissen?»

«Da sind schwarze Wolken.»

«Unser Anzeichen dafür, dass etwas passieren wird.»

«Genau. Lass mich das nochmal wiederholen, bevor wir weitermachen. Ich mach auch gleich eine kleine Tabelle, und du sagst mir dann, was du davon hältst.»

ZEITFORM	VERWENDUNG	BEISPIEL
Simple Future Will-Future (Futur I)	bei einfachen Aussagen	I'll be here until 10 o'clock.
Simple Future Will-Future (Futur I)	bei spontanen Entscheidungen	In that case I'll have some pop tarts instead.
Going-to-Future	zum Ausdruck von Plänen für die Zukunft	I'm going to kick your head in!
Going-to-Future	zum Ausdruck von Ereignissen, die man als logische Folge von etwas betrachtet	Wayne is going to fail the course!

"Like it?"

"Like it? I love it, Barry. In fact I'll copy it and give it out to my students."

"Let's get back to more serious things. It's not too long before I'm off to sunny Germany."

"Good point and we still have another four forms to look at."

"Another four?"

"Well, we've only looked at 'will' future and 'going to' future so far. But, if you're weary and feeling small we don't have to finish it all today. What about tomorrow?"

"Can't."

"Why not?"

"*I'm seeing* Susan in the pub tomorrow."

"I don't believe you!"

"It's true! Look, here's my *diary*. Thursday, seven o'clock: see Susan in the pub. Why have you got that smile on your face?"

"Because you just used the next form."

"I did?"

"You certainly did. When we talk about *arrangements* that we have made with a few other people, the kind of *arrangement* that you would write in your *diary* …"

"Like seeing Susan in the pub?"

"Exactly like that. Do you remember what you told me earlier? Why can't you see me tomorrow?"

« Und? Gefällt dir die Tabelle? »

« Gefallen? Ich finde sie klasse, Barry. Ich werde sie gleich mal kopieren und meinen Schülern geben. »

« Lass uns nun aber über wichtigere Dinge sprechen. Es ist nicht mehr lange hin, bis ich ins sonnige Deutschland fahre. »

« Gute Idee. Wir müssen uns auch noch vier weitere Zeitformen vornehmen. »

« Nochmals vier? »

« Ja. Wir haben bisher nur Simple Future und das Going-to-Future besprochen. Aber wenn du müde bist und keine Lust mehr hast, dann brauchen wir heute nicht alles durchzugehen. Wie sieht es morgen aus? »

« Da kann ich nicht. »

« Warum nicht? »

« Da geh ich mit Susan in eine Kneipe. »

« Wirklich? »

« Ja, wirklich. Schau, in meinem Kalender steht's. Donnerstag sieben Uhr: Treffen mit Susan in der Kneipe. Warum grinst du so? »

« Weil du eben eine weitere Form verwendet hast. »

« Hab ich? »

« Ja, das hast du. Wir nehmen sie, um auszudrücken, dass etwas geplant ist, dass wir etwas mit anderen Leuten abgesprochen haben, also für Dinge, die wir in unseren Kalender schreiben würden. »

« Etwa ‹ Treffen mit Susan in der Kneipe ›? »

« Genau das. Erinnerst du dich noch daran, was du mir vorher gesagt hast? Also, warum du mich morgen nicht treffen kannst? »

"Because *I'm seeing* Susan in the pub tomorrow!"

"Exactly!"

"But wait a minute, that's the *present continuous* form. Surely I shouldn't've used that for a future form!"

"Have a little more faith in your own English, Barry. We do use the *present continuous with future meaning* if we are talking about an *arrangement* that we have made. The kind of thing you would write in your *diary*. In fact many people call it '*diary future*'."

"Okay, got that. I'll remember to keep an eye on my diary. Next please!"

"You sound like someone selling tickets in a train station!"

"I used to live near a train station you know."

«Weil ich mich morgen mit Susan in einer Kneipe treffe?»

«Genau!»

«Wart mal kurz. Ich habe dafür das Present Continuous benutzt. Das hätte ich wohl nicht tun sollen, oder?»

«Hab doch ein bisschen mehr Vertrauen in dich, Barry, dein Englisch ist gut! Wir verwenden Present Continuous für Abmachungen über Ereignisse in der Zukunft. Also für Dinge, die du in deinen Kalender schreiben würdest. Genaugenommen sprechen viele auch vom Diary Future.»

«Okay, das habe ich verstanden. Lass mal sehen, was sonst noch in meinem Kalender steht. Der nächste bitte!»

«Du hörst dich an, als ob du Fahrkarten verkaufen würdest.»

«Weißt du, ich habe früher in der Nähe eines Bahnhofs gewohnt.»

"How convenient. I'm going to Bristol on Saturday. Can you tell me the time of the first train from London to Bristol please?"

"No problem. That *timetable* is branded into my poor brain cells. The first train to Bristol leaves at quarter past six."

"On Saturday."

"Yes, on Saturday."

"You mean in three days' time."

"Yes, in three days' time. Are you a little slow? Bad at mathematics perhaps?"

"No, no. I'm just checking. Making sure that you realise that you are talking about the future."

"Again? What did I say?"

"You said, The first train to Bristol leaves at quarter past six."

"But that's the *present simple tense*! We use that for things which happen on a regular basis."

"Well, surely the 06.15 to Bristol leaves on a regular basis – every Saturday."

"Well, it would if the service wasn't so crap."

"The important thing is that the 06.15 train is on a *timetable*. On some kind of *fixed agenda*. In such cases we can use the *simple present tense* although we are talking about an event in the future."

"I've got you. But it isn't a very common form, is it?"

« Wie praktisch. Ich fahre am Samstag nach Bristol. Könntest du mir bitte sagen, wann der erste Zug von London nach Bristol geht? »

« Kein Problem. Der Fahrplan hat sich in meine Hirnzellen eingebrannt. Der erste Zug nach Bristol geht um Viertel nach sechs. »

« Am Samstag? »

« Ja, am Samstag. »

« Also in drei Tagen? »

« Ja, in drei Tagen. Bist du heute etwas schwer von Begriff? Oder schlecht in Mathe? »

« Nein, nein. Ich wollte nur herausfinden, ob dir auch wirklich bewusst ist, dass du über die Zukunft sprichst. »

« Schon wieder? Was habe ich gesagt? »

« Du hast gesagt, der erste Zug nach Bristol geht um Viertel nach sechs. »

« Aber das ist das Simple Present. Nehmen wir nicht diese Gegenwartsform für Dinge, die regelmäßig geschehen? »

« Ja genau! Der 6-Uhr-15-Zug nach Bristol fährt regelmäßig jeden Samstag. »

« Sollte er. Tut er aber nicht. Der Service ist viel zu lausig. »

« Wichtig ist, dass der 6-Uhr-15-Zug auf dem Fahrplan steht, sozusagen ein fester Zeitpunkt ist. In solchen Fällen können wir das Simple Present nehmen, obwohl wir über etwas reden, das in der Zukunft liegt. »

« Habe verstanden. Aber es ist nicht unbedingt eine sehr gebräuchliche Form, oder? »

"Well if you join the army then you'll hear it a lot. Our plans for tomorrow: We get up at five. We march for six hours. We stop for lunch. We go on an assault course …"

"That sounds like a bag of laughs! But as I'm not planning to join the army and I don't live near a railway station any more I don't think I'm going to hear this form that often."

"True, we are looking at the various forms in order of frequency. This one is number six out of eight that we are going to look at to-day."

"Aha, 'going to' future! You're telling me your plan or intention!"

"I'm glad you're listening."

"So, just two more to go! I really want to finish this. I'm going away on Saturday."

"Going away? Where are you going?"

"To the Cairngorm mountains. Ah yes, on Saturday afternoon *I'll be sitting* on top of Ben Nevis, eating my cheese and pickle sand-wiches …"

"Perfect!"

"Not really, I'd rather have a pot noodle but it's a real hassle …"

"No, I mean your example."

"My example?"

"Of the *future continuous*!"

"All I said was 'eating my cheese and pickle sandwiches'."

« Wenn du beim Militär wärst, würdest du diese Form ziemlich häufig hören. Unsere Pläne für morgen: um fünf Uhr aufstehen, sechs Stunden marschieren, eine kleine Mittagspause, dann auf das Übungsgelände ... »

« Lustig! Aber da ich nicht vorhabe, zur Armee zu gehen, und ich auch nicht mehr in der Nähe eines Bahnhofs wohne, werde ich diese Form wohl nicht zu oft hören. »

« Das ist wohl wahr. Wir schauen uns die verschiedenen Zukunftsformen abhängig von deren Häufigkeit an. Dies ist die sechste von den acht, die wir heute durchgehen werden. »

« Aha, das Going-to-Future. Du erzählst mir von einem Plan oder einer Absicht. »

« Freut mich, dass du mir zuhörst. »

« Also nur noch zwei! Ich will damit fertig werden. Ich werde am Samstag verreisen. »

« Verreisen? Wo soll es denn hingehen? »

« In das Cairngorm-Gebirge. Ja, und am Samstagnachmittag werde ich dann auf dem Ben Nevis sitzen und mir belegte Brötchen mit Käse und Essiggürkchen schmecken lassen. »

« Hervorragend! »

« Nicht unbedingt. Mir wäre eine 5-Minuten-Terrine lieber; aber das wäre zu viel Aufwand. »

« Nein. Ich meine doch dein Beispiel. »

« Mein Beispiel? »

« Zum Future Continuous! »

« Alles, was ich gesagt habe, war, dass ich ein belegtes Brötchen essen werde. »

"No, no, before that."

"*I'll be sitting* on top of Ben Nevis …"

"Exactly! When you look to the future and tell someone about an action at a particular time in the future, you use the future continuous! Tell me, *what will you be doing* at three o'clock tomorrow morning?"

"Sleeping, if I'm lucky, or perhaps not sleeping if I'm lucky!"

"Forget the smut, Barry, and give me a full answer!"

"Sorry, oh great master. '*I'll be sleeping* at three o'clock tomorrow morning.' Okay?"

"So you started the action of sleeping some time before three o'clock?"

"Probably."

"And continued it some time after three o'clock?"

"Probably. Good grief, you sound like a bloody policeman!"

"I'm just asking some checking questions. Making sure that you understand when to use the *future continuous*."

"In a few months' time *I'll be sitting* in a classroom in Germany, helping the poor Germans understand how to talk about things in the future."

"Though don't be surprised if your students know a lot more about grammar than you do. In Britain we're not taught how our grammar

«Nein, nicht das. Vorher.»

«Dass ich auf dem Ben Nevis sitzen werde.»

«Genau das! Wenn du jemandem von einer Handlung erzählst, die zu einem bestimmten Zeitpunkt stattfinden wird, dann verwendest du Future Continuous! Sag mal, was machst du morgen früh um drei Uhr?»

«Wenn ich Glück habe, schlafe ich, oder eben auch nicht!»

«Lass deine Zweideutigkeiten, Barry, und sag lieber einen vollständigen Satz.»

«Entschuldigung, großer Meister. Morgen früh um drei Uhr werde ich schlafen. Besser so?»

«Du wirst mit der Handlung, also dem Schlafen, bereits vor drei Uhr begonnen haben, oder?»

«Wahrscheinlich.»

«Und wirst auch nach drei Uhr noch weiterschlafen?»

«Wahrscheinlich. Ach, du meine Güte, das ist ja wie in einem Verhör!»

«Ich stelle nur ein paar Kontrollfragen, um herauszufinden, ob du verstanden hast, wann du das Future Continuous verwenden musst.»

«In einigen Monaten werde ich in einem Klassenzimmer in Deutschland stehen und meinen armen Englischschülern beibringen, wie sie über in der Zukunft liegende Dinge reden sollen.»

«Wundere dich aber nicht, wenn deine Schüler deutlich mehr Grammatik können als du. Hier in Großbritannien lernen wir nichts über unsere Grammatik. Das

works. It's a bit like driving a car – in Britain most people can drive but they don't have much of an idea what is going on under the bonnet."

"I'm afraid you've lost me there. But the *future continuous* was number seven. Now to the final one! This one must be really exotic. Surely no one ever uses the eighth one."

"You'd be surprised. How many countries have you visited?"

"Me? I'm a great traveller. I've visited ninety-nine countries!"

"Any travel plans this summer?"

"Yeah, I'm off to North Korea with Aunt Rosemary."

"How convenient. Been before, have you?"

"Nope!"

"So at the moment you have visited ninety-nine countries. But by September ..."

"I *will have visited* a hundred countries!"

"Amazing!"

"Am I?"

"Not you, me! I elicited all eight forms out of you."

"But where was number eight? I *won't have gained* a full understanding of futurity until I hear the eighth one!"

"There it is again!"

"There is what again?"

"The future perfect! You are looking ahead

ist ungefähr so wie beim Autofahren. In Großbritannien können die meisten Leute Auto fahren, haben aber dennoch keine Ahnung von dem, was unter der Haube vor sich geht.»

«Nun versteh ich nur noch Bahnhof. Aber das Future Continuous war dann Nummer sieben. Eine noch! Das muss dann wohl eine ziemlich exotische Form sein. Wahrscheinlich eine, die niemals benutzt wird.»

«Wart's ab. In wie vielen Ländern bist du schon gewesen?»

«Ich? Ich bin viel rumgekommen. Ich war bereits in neunundneunzig Ländern.»

«Und wo soll's diesen Sommer hingehen?»

«Diesen Sommer fliege ich mit Tante Rosemary nach Nordkorea.»

«Wie nett. Warst du da schon mal?»

«Ne!»

«Du warst also schon in neunundneunzig Ländern. Und im September …»

«… werde ich hundert Länder besucht haben.»

«Großartig!»

«Bin ich das?»

«Nicht du, ich! Ich habe dir quasi alle acht Futurformen entlockt.»

«Aber was ist nun die achte? Was ‹Zukünftigkeit› angeht, werde ich den vollen Durchblick erst haben, wenn ich alle acht Formen kenne.»

«Da ist es wieder!»

«Da ist was wieder?»

«Das Future Perfect! Das benutzt du, wenn du dich

to a time in the future but then you are looking back from that time."

"That sounds wickedly complicated."

"It's not easy but you'd be surprised how often we use it."

"Hmm, can I produce a little table like last time?"

"Be my guest."

"Okay, that's it. All eight forms."

"Well …"

"Well what?"

"Well there are a few others and then there are many cases in which you could use quite a few different forms but I didn't want to make it complicated for you."

auf etwas beziehst, das in der Zukunft liegt, da aber bereits stattgefunden hat. »

« Das hört sich furchtbar kompliziert an. »

« Es ist nicht gerade einfach, aber du wirst dich wundern, wie oft wir es benutzen. »

« Hm. Kann ich auch wieder eine Tabelle machen, so wie für die anderen Zukunftsformen? »

« Gerne. »

ZEITFORM	WIRD VERWENDET, WENN	BEISPIEL
Present Continuous	… über Abmachungen/ Verabredungen gesprochen wird (Diary Future)	I'm seeing Susan in the pub tomorrow at five o'clock.
Simple Present	… über sich wiederholende Vorgänge gesprochen wird (Timetable Future)	The first train to Bristol leaves at quarter past six.
Future Continuous	… über eine Handlung gesprochen wird, die zu einer bestimmten Zeit in der Zukunft stattfindet	Tomorrow afternoon I'll be sitting on top of Ben Nevis …
Future Perfect	… über eine in der Zukunft abgeschlossene Handlung gesprochen wird	By September I will have visited hundred countries.

« Okay. Das waren alle acht Formen. »

« Ja, das waren die acht, aber … »

« Was aber? »

« Nun, da gibt es noch ein paar andere, und dann gibt es Fälle, bei denen du andere Zeitformen verwenden könntest. Aber ich wollte es nicht zu kompliziert machen. »

"Not complicated ! ! ! Come here. I'm going to give you a good slap."

"Aha ! 'Going to' future used because of … OW! OW! OW!"

« Nicht kompliziert ! ! ! Komm doch mal her. Es gibt gleich einen Satz heiße Ohren. »

« Aha. Da hast du das Going-to-Future benutzt, weil … Autsch ! Autsch ! Autsch ! »

Simple Present or Present Continuous? That Is the Question

"I've got a little quiz for you today, Barry."

"Treeeeeemendous! I love quizzes, me!"

"Does the earth go around the sun or does the sun go around the earth?"

"Ha! I know that one! It looks like the sun goes around the earth, but actually the earth goes around the sun!"

"Excellent! Do you know how long it takes?"

"I'm not sure. It must take years!"

"Actually it takes approximately three hundred and sixty-five and a quarter days."

"Unlucky! It would be much easier to calculate things if it took exactly a year."

Simple Present oder Present Continuous, das ist hier die Frage

«Heute habe ich eine kleine Denksportaufgabe für dich, Barry.»

«Herrrrlich! Das ist was für mich!»

«Dreht sich die Erde um die Sonne, oder dreht sich die Sonne um die Erde?»

«Ha! Das weiß ich! Es sieht so aus, als ob die Sonne um die Erde kreist, aber es ist tatsächlich die Erde, die um die Sonne kreist.»

«Ausgezeichnet! Und weißt du auch, wie lange das dauert?»

«Ich bin mir nicht sicher. Das dauert sicher Jahre!»

«Das dauert genau dreihundertfünfundsechzig Tage und sechs Stunden.»

«Das ist nicht gut! Es wäre viel einfacher zu rechnen, wenn es genau ein Jahr dauern würde.»

"Hmm. Okay, another question. What do lions eat?"

"Meat! They're carnivorous animals!"

"Four syllables. Well done. Are you thinking of any *particular* lions? The ones you saw in the zoo last week for example?"

"No, you didn't tell me to think about any *specific* lions – only *lions in general.*"

"Very good. How often do lions eat?"

"Specific lions or lions in general?"

"Lions in general."

"I'm not sure. I would think once or twice a week."

"Fine. What about sheep?"

"What about them?"

"I mean, what do sheep eat?"

"Oh, that's an easy one: grass! In fact, did you know that sheep eat grass for eighteen hours a day?"

"No, I have to admit that that fact had eluded me until now."

"It's true."

"Very interesting. Now what about your mother?"

"She eats lots of different things, pop tarts, pot noodles …"

"Okay, but I'm interested in her daily *routine*. What does she do every day?"

"She gets up at about half past six, has a quick shower, grabs a quick pot noodle and then prepares breakfast for me, my dad, my brother and

«Hm. Also gut. Noch eine Frage. Was fressen Löwen?»

«Fleisch! Löwen sind Karnivoren.»

«Vier Silben, prima! Denkst du an bestimmte Löwen? Zum Beispiel an die, die du letzte Woche im Zoo gesehen hast?»

«Nein, du hast nicht gesagt, dass ich an bestimmte Löwen denken soll – nur an Löwen ganz allgemein.»

«Sehr gut. Wie oft fressen Löwen?»

«Bestimmte Löwen oder Löwen ganz allgemein?»

«Löwen ganz allgemein.»

«Da bin ich mir nicht sicher. Ich denke, so ein- bis zweimal die Woche.»

«Gut. Und was ist mit Schafen?»

«Was soll mit ihnen sein?»

«Ich meine, was fressen sie?»

«Ach so, das ist einfach. Gras! Wusstest du eigentlich, dass Schafe achtzehn Stunden am Tag Gras fressen?»

«Nein. Ich muss zugeben, dass ich das bisher nicht wusste.»

«Stimmt aber.»

«Sehr interessant. Und deine Mutter?»

«Sie isst viele verschiedene Sachen, Pop-Tarts, 5-Minuten-Terrine ...»

«Gut, aber ich will eher etwas über ihre tägliche Routine wissen. Was macht sie jeden Tag?»

«Sie steht um halb sieben auf, duscht schnell, packt eine 5-Minuten-Terrine ein und macht dann Frühstück für mich, meinen Vater, meinen Bruder und

sister. Then, at about half past eight she heads off to the bank. She works there all day and then comes home and cleans the house and then prepares dinner for the whole family. She goes to bed at about nine o'clock."

"She works pretty hard. I hope you help her."

"Me? No, I'm far too busy."

"Hmm. Okay, is that your mum's daily *routine*?"

"It is."

"Things she does on a regular basis?"

"Every day – except Sunday."

"So what happens on Sunday?"

"We let her stay in bed for an extra half an hour and, of course, she doesn't go to the bank."

"So what does she do?"

meine Schwester. Um halb neun geht sie in die Bank. Sie arbeitet dort den Tag über, kommt nachhause, putzt das Haus und macht anschließend Abendessen für die ganze Familie. Gegen neun Uhr geht sie zu Bett. »

« Sie arbeitet ziemlich viel. Ich hoffe, du hilfst ihr. »

« Ich? Nein, ich bin viel zu beschäftigt. »

« Hm. Und das alles macht deine Mutter jeden Tag? »

« Ja. »

« Also regelmäßig jeden Tag? »

« Jeden Tag – außer sonntags. »

« Was ist am Sonntag? »

« Da darf sie eine halbe Stunde länger im Bett bleiben, und natürlich geht sie auch nicht in die Bank. »

« Was macht sie stattdessen? »

"She works in the garden all morning. We've got a huge garden and it needs a lot of work done on it."

"Hmm. Do you help her?"

"Well, I would but it clashes."

"What does it clash with?"

"The repeat of Match of the Day. I can't miss that."

"So *every Sunday* your poor mother works in the garden."

"Correct."

"*On a regular basis.*"

"Come rain or shine."

"Unbelievable."

"Um, excuse me. Is there some point to this? We had a little quiz and now you're asking about my mother and her *routines and habits.*"

"What an excellent choice of words."

"Which ones?"

"*Routines and habits.* The earth goes around the sun on a *regular basis.* Lions eat meat. Sheep eat grass …"

"For eighteen hours a day!"

"We're talking about things *in general. Regular things and habits.*"

"And?"

"When talking about such things we use the *simple present.*"

"The what?"

"The *simple present.* It is a present tense

« Sie arbeitet den ganzen Morgen im Garten. Wir haben einen riesigen Garten, der ganz schön viel Arbeit macht. »

« Hm. Hilfst du ihr bei dieser Arbeit? »

« Na ja, ich würde ja gerne, aber es passt nicht. »

« Warum das denn? »

« Da kommt die Sportschau. Die darf ich nicht versäumen. »

« Deine arme Mutter arbeitet also jeden Sonntag im Garten? »

« Ja. »

« Regelmäßig. »

« Egal, ob es regnet oder schneit. »

« Das ist ja kaum zu glauben. »

« Warte mal. Was soll das Ganze? Wir haben mit einem kleinen Frage-und-Antwort-Spiel begonnen, und nun sind wir bei meiner Mutter, ihren Routinen und Gepflogenheiten. »

« Was für eine ausgezeichnete Wortwahl! »

« Welche Wortwahl meinst du? »

« Routinen und Gepflogenheiten. Die Erde dreht sich regelmäßig um die Sonne. Löwen fressen Fleisch. Schafe fressen Gras … »

« Achtzehn Stunden lang! »

« Es geht hier um Dinge ganz allgemein. Dinge, die regelmäßig geschehen, oder auch Gewohnheiten. »

« Und? »

« Wenn wir über solche Dinge reden, verwenden wir das Simple Present. »

« Das was? »

« Das Simple Present. Das ist eine Gegenwartsform,

form but we only use it for *things in general, things which occur on a regular basis.*"

"Like the earth going around the sun!"

"Exactly."

"You said, 'a present tense form'. Is there another one?"

"There certainly is. How are you feeling today?"

"Me? Grand. Why?"

"Just wondered. I like that jacket you're wearing. That lime green shirt goes very nicely with your yellow tie."

"I'm glad you like it."

"What's your sister, Emma, doing these days?"

"She's got a new job! She's working in that new supermarket; she's a cashier."

"Do you think she'll be there for a long time?"

"I doubt it. She hates it and her boss is a creep."

"Interesting. Is she married yet?"

"Not yet. She's waiting for Mr Right! Ha ha.

CONTINUOUS . . . .

die wir allerdings nur für allgemeine Aussagen, Dinge, die sich wiederholen, verwenden.»

«Dass die Erde um die Sonne kreist zum Beispiel!»

«Richtig.»

«Du hast gesagt, eine Gegenwartsform. Gibt es noch andere?»

«Auf jeden Fall. Wie geht es dir heute?»

«Mir? Super. Warum?»

«Nur so. Mir gefällt deine Jacke. Das limetten-grüne Hemd passt ganz gut zu deiner gelben Krawatte.»

«Freut mich, dass es dir gefällt.»

«Was macht eigentlich deine Schwester Emma?»

«Sie hat eine neue Arbeitsstelle. Sie arbeitet zur Zeit als Kassiererin in dem neuen Supermarkt.»

«Denkst du, sie wird dort länger arbeiten?»

«Das bezweifle ich. Sie hasst die Arbeit, und ihr Boss ist ein ziemlicher Fiesling.»

«Interessant. Ist sie schon verheiratet?»

«Noch nicht. Sie wartet noch auf den Richtigen. Haha!»

I reckon she'll still be looking in twenty years time!"

"Very interesting. One more question …"

"It feels like the Spanish inquisition this morning!"

"If you don't mind …"

"Go ahead, oh great master."

"Are you into books?"

"That's a bit of funny question."

"I admit, it's a bit colloquial."

"Colloquial? What does that mean when it's at home?"

"Any informal use of the language. 'What does that mean *when it's at home?*' for example. Anyway back to my question. Are you into books?"

"Me? Yeah, I'm into books, me. In fact I'm reading a dead good book *at the moment*."

"Really? What's it called?"

"'An Arrow Full of Quivers'."

"I think you mean 'A Quiver Full of Arrows'."

"That's the one. It's brilliant, a real page turner."

"Jeffrey Archer is not my sort of thing I'm afraid."

"Good joke! I like that one!"

"Joke? What joke?"

"Archer! Quiver Full of Arrows! Nice one!"

"Very drôle. Anyway, where's your book?"

"What book?"

"The 'brilliant' 'Quiver Full of Arrows'."

Ich denke, auf den wird sie auch noch in zwanzig Jahren warten.»

«Sehr interessant. Noch eine Frage … »

«Es fühlt sich heute an wie bei der Spanischen Inquisition!»

«Wenn es dir nichts ausmacht … »

«Mach einfach weiter, großer Meister.»

«Bist du nicht eine Leseratte?»

«Das ist eine etwas komische Frage.»

«Zugegeben, etwas kolloquial.»

«Kolloquial? Was bedeutet das denn schon wieder?»

«Das ist jeder informelle Gebrauch von Sprache, etwa ‹What does that mean when it's at home?›. Egal, zurück zu meiner Frage, ob du eine Leseratte bist.»

«Ich? Ja, ich denke schon. Ich lese zum Beispiel gerade ein megagutes Buch.»

«Wirklich? Wie heißt es?»

«‹Ein Pfeil voller Köcher›.»

«Du meinst wohl ‹Ein Köcher voller Pfeile›.»

«Stimmt, so heißt es. Ein echter Schmöker.»

«Tut mir leid, aber Jeffrey Archer ist nicht unbedingt mein Fall.»

«Das ist ein guter Witz! Der gefällt mir!»

«Witz? Welcher Witz?»

«Bogenschütze! Köcher voller Pfeile! Gefällt mir!»

«Sehr witzig. Egal, wo ist dein Buch?»

«Welches Buch?»

«‹Ein Köcher voller Pfeiler›, das dir so gefällt.»

"Oh it's at home. Do you want to borrow it? I can lend …"

"Er, thanks, but no thanks. But you've started the book but you haven't finished it yet."

"That's right. I'm on page 14 but I've only had it out of the library for a week."

"A real page turner."

"It is! It is! But wait a minute. I'm here to learn about English grammar, not to talk about books!"

"There is method in my madness."

"I acknowledge your superior wisdom from the heart of my bottom."

"Hmm, anyway, we're looking at present tense forms today."

"We are?"

"Indeed we are. Not *yesterday*, not *tomorrow*, but *right now, at the moment.*"

"Yes, I think I understand you. I may not understand the intricacies of the English language

54

«Oh ja, das habe ich zuhause. Willst du es ausleihen? Ich kann es …»

«Ich glaube nicht. Aber trotzdem danke. Hast du nicht gerade erst mit dem Buch angefangen?»

«Stimmt. Aber ich bin schon auf Seite 14. Ich habe es erst vor einer Woche ausgeliehen.»

«Ein echter Schmöker.»

«Ja genau! Ist es! Aber warte mal. Ich bin hier, um etwas über englische Grammatik zu lernen, nicht, um über Bücher zu reden!»

«Meine Methode hat System.»

«Ich schätze deine überlegene Weisheit aus dem Herzen meiner Tiefe.»

«Hm, auch egal, wir sind gerade bei der Gegenwartsform.»

«Tatsächlich?»

«Und ob. Nicht gestern, nicht morgen, sondern jetzt gerade, in diesem Moment.»

«Ich denke, ich verstehe, was du meinst. Ich verstehe womöglich nicht die Feinheiten der englischen Sprache,

but I can speak the language and I understand most of what you say."

"That's good but I am trying to emphasize something. *Right now, over a comparatively short period of time.*"

"Keep going."

"Okay, let's look at your stylish clothes."

"My lime green shirt and my yellow tie!"

"Exactly. Did you wear them yesterday?"

"No I didn't!"

"I'm not questioning your personal hygiene; I'm just asking checking questions."

"That's all right then."

"Are you going to wear them tomorrow?"

"Not me. I wear something different every day."

"A bit like the Queen."

"Yes, I've noticed she does that as well."

"So *at the moment,* and for a *comparatively short period of time, you are wearing* a lime green shirt and a yellow tie."

"And proud of it!"

"Fine. We now have an excellent example of the *present continuous.*"

"The what?"

"The *present continuous.*"

"What's the present continuous when it's at home?"

"It's the name of the English tense we use when we are talking about things *at the mo-*

aber ich kann sie sprechen, und ich verstehe das meiste von dem, was du sagst.»

«Gut so, aber ich versuche etwas hervorzuheben. Jetzt gerade, in einer vergleichsweise kurzen Zeit.»

«Weiter.»

«Gut. Schauen wir uns deine stilvolle Kleidung an.»

«Mein limettengrünes Hemd und meine gelbe Krawatte!»

«Genau. Hattest du das gestern auch schon an?»

«Nein, das hatte ich nicht!»

«Ich stelle nicht deine Hygienestandards infrage. Ich stelle nur Fragen, um mich zu vergewissern.»

«Dann ist es ja gut.»

«Ziehst du diese Sachen morgen an?»

«Nein! Ich ziehe jeden Tag etwas anderes an.»

«Ein bisschen wie die Königin, oder?»

«Stimmt, mir ist auch aufgefallen, dass sie das macht.»

«Das bedeutet, dass du in diesem Moment und für einen relativ kurzen Zeitraum ein limettengrünes Hemd und eine gelbe Krawatte trägst.»

«Und ich bin stolz darauf!»

«Gut. Das war ein sehr schönes Beispiel für das Present Continuous.»

«Das was?»

«Das Present Continuous.»

«Und was soll das sein, dieses Present Continuous, bitte schön?»

«So nennt man die englische Zeitform, die man benutzt, wenn man über Handlungen spricht, die im

ment, things which can be considered *tempo-rary in nature, occurring over a comparatively short period of time."*

"Like me and my lime green shirt and my yellow tie !"

"Exactly."

"But what is 'continuous'? I'm only going to wear it for another few hours."

"I admit that 'continuous' is not a good name for the tense. Please don't hold me responsible for the illogicality of the English language. You will find many English tenses are called the *** continuous. There's the past continuous – and maybe you remember the future continuous. All of them end in -ing."

"You mean like : *'I am wearing* a lime green shirt and a yellow tie.'?"

"Exactly. Some people call this form the *present progressive."*

"That doesn't help very much. It reminds me of progressive schools where you don't have to go to lessons if you don't want to."

"True, but can you think of a more satisfactory name?"

"How about the *'at the moment, temporary in nature, occurring over a comparatively short period of time'* form?"

"I'll stick with present continuous if you don't mind."

"Suit yourself."

Moment des Sprechens oder die nur vorübergehend, also während eines relativ kurzen Zeitraums, stattfinden.»

«Dass ich gerade ein limettengrünes Hemd und eine gelbe Krawatte trage?»

«Genau»

«Aber was meinst du mit ‹continuous›? Ich trage das doch nur noch für ein paar Stunden.»

«Zugegebenermaßen ist ‹continous› nicht gerade die beste Bezeichnung für diese Zeitform. Aber mach mich bitte nicht für die mangelnde Logik der englischen Sprache verantwortlich. Es gibt zahlreiche englische Zeitformen, die *** Continuous heißen. Past Continuous zum Beispiel, oder erinnere dich an das Future Continuous. Alle Verben enden dabei auf -ing.»

«Meinst du so was wie ‹Ich trage ein limettengrünes Hemd und eine gelbe Krawatte›?»

«Richtig. Manche nennen diese Zeitform auch Present Progressive.»

«Das hilft mir nicht weiter. Das erinnert mich an progressive Schulen, wo man nicht zum Unterricht erscheinen muss, wenn man nicht will.»

«Stimmt wohl. Welchen Namen würdest du vorschlagen?»

«Was hältst du von ‹Zeitform, die im Moment passierende, vorübergehende Handlungen, die nur während eines kurzen Zeitraums stattfinden, beschreibt›?»

«Wenn's dir nichts ausmacht, bleibe ich doch lieber bei Present Continuous.»

«Wie du willst.»

"Now when you are teaching the present continuous to foreign learners, they often have problems."

"Are they a bit stupid?"

"Not at all. English is one of the few languages which has two present tenses. Many foreigners find it annoying that we have two different forms."

"How cheeky!"

"When learning a new language it is very important to accept differences and not get flustered when the language is not identical in structure to your own."

"One in the eye for the foreigners!"

"I was thinking more of speakers of English. We are pretty pathetic when it comes to foreign languages."

"Not me! Voulez-vous couchon avec moi, sir soir?"

"I rest my case."

"Why? What was wrong with that?"

"I'll tell you later. Now, tell me a little about your brother."

"Jason. He's a bit of a boring guy. He works in an insurance company. Got his whole life planned out."

"So Jason's employment could be considered *a pretty permanent fixture.*"

"As permanent a fixture as the Rock of Gibraltar!"

«Du wirst als Fremdsprachenlehrer merken, dass viele deiner Schüler Probleme mit dieser Zeitform haben.»

«Sind die ein bisschen dumm?»

«Nein, absolut nicht. Englisch ist eine der wenigen Sprachen, die zwei Gegenwartsformen haben. Viele Leute aus anderen Ländern finden es ziemlich nervig, dass wir zwei unterschiedliche Formen haben.»

«Wie frech!»

«Beim Erlernen einer neuen Sprache ist es sehr wichtig, Unterschiede zu akzeptieren und sich nicht verwirren zu lassen, wenn die Struktur der neuen Sprache nicht der der eigenen entspricht.»

«Denen sollte man eins auf die Nase geben!»

«Ich dachte da eher an die englischen Muttersprachler. Wir stellen uns ziemlich miserabel an, wenn es um das Erlernen anderer Sprachen geht.»

«Ich nicht! Voulez-vous couchon avec moi, sir soir?»

«Genau.»

«Warum? Was ist jetzt wieder falsch?»

«Ich sag's dir später. Erzähl mir lieber was von deinem Bruder.»

«Jason? Er ist ein ziemlicher Langweiler. Er arbeitet bei einer Versicherung und hat sein ganzes Leben durchgeplant.»

«Jasons Anstellung könnte daher als ziemlich beständig angesehen werden.»

«Ja, so fest und unverrückbar wie der Fels von Gibraltar!»

"I wouldn't use that example if you have any Spanish students. Now let's compare Jason, the boring fellow, with your sister, Emma. What did you tell me about her earlier?"

"She's working in that new supermarket. You've got a lousy memory."

"Not true, I'm simply eliciting information from you. Now you have two siblings."

"Siblings? You mean my brothers and sisters?"

"That's right. Anyway, you spoke about the employment status of your brother Jason and your sister Emma."

"My 'siblings'!"

"Don't snigger. It doesn't suit a professional English teacher."

"Sorry, oh great one."

"Your apology is accepted. Now, back to Jason and Emma. Now your exact words were: She's working in that new supermarket. Then later you said, and I quote: He works in an insurance company."

"And?"

"You used the two different forms, the present continuous and the simple present although you were talking about essentially the same thing, the work done by each of your siblings."

"Call me stupid if you want to, but I'm afraid I'm a little lost at the moment."

«Ich würde dieses Beispiel nicht unbedingt bei spanischen Schülern verwenden. Lass uns jetzt einmal Jason, also den Langweiler, mit deiner Schwester Emma vergleichen. Was hast du mir vorher über sie gesagt?»

«Dass sie in diesem neuen Supermarkt arbeitet. Du hast aber ein schlechtes Gedächtnis!»

«Stimmt nicht. Ich versuche nur, dir Informationen zu entlocken. Du hast also zwei Geschwister.»

«Geschwister? Du meinst meinen Bruder und meine Schwester?»

«Ja. Aber egal. Du hast gerade von dem Beschäftigungsverhältnis deines Bruders Jason und dem deiner Schwester Emma gesprochen.»

«Ja, das sind meine Geschwister!»

«Mach dich nicht lustig. Das steht einem professionellen Englischlehrer nicht zu.»

«Entschuldigung, mein Meister.»

«Entschuldigung angenommen! Aber nun zurück zu Jason und Emma. Deine genauen Worte waren: Sie arbeitet (‹she is working›) in dem neuen Supermarkt. Später sagtest du dann, und ich zitiere: Er arbeitet (‹he works›) bei einer Versicherung.»

«Und?»

«Du hast zwei verschiedene Formen verwendet, das Present Continuous und das Simple Present, und das, obwohl du von ein und demselben gesprochen hast, nämlich der Arbeit deiner beiden Geschwister.»

«Halte mich gerne für dumm, aber im Moment versteh ich wirklich nur Bahnhof.»

"I would never call any student of mine 'stupid'. I shoulder the responsibility for not having explained it clearly enough."

"You must have pretty broad shoulders then."

"Perhaps. You said: 'She's working in that new supermarket.'"

"Present continuous! – I recognized that because of the -ing bit at the end."

"Then you said: 'He works in an insurance company.'"

"He works! That's the other one, the simple present!"

"Correct!"

"But surely for something like that I should have used the same form."

"Have more faith in your own English. You used them correctly. I am trying my best to open your eyes to the wondrous complexities of the English language."

"I agree with the complexity bit, I'm not so sure about the 'wondrous'!"

"Back to your example. You mentioned that Emma probably won't be at the supermarket for long."

"True, I'd give her about a week."

"So her work there could be considered of a temporary nature."

"Present continuous!"

"There was a slight jump in logic there but I think you jumped in the right direction."

«Ich würde niemals einen meiner Schüler ‹dumm›
nennen. Die Verantwortung dafür, dass ich das nicht gut
genug erklärt habe, lastet allein auf meinen Schultern.»

«Dann musst du ziemlich breite Schultern haben.»

«Vielleicht. Du hast gesagt, ‹sie arbeitet in dem neuen
Supermarkt›, und hast dabei ‹she is working› benutzt.»

«Present Continuous! Ich habe das an der ing-Form
erkannt.»

«Und dann hast du gesagt: ‹Er arbeitet bei einer Versicherung›, also ‹he works›.»

«He works! Das ist die andere Zeitform, das Simple
Present!»

«Stimmt genau!»

«Aber wahrscheinlich hätte ich die gleiche Zeitform
verwenden sollen.»

«Vertrau doch deinem Sprachgefühl. Du hast alles
richtig gemacht. Ich versuche nur mein Bestes, dir die
Augen für die wunderbare Komplexität der englischen
Sprache zu öffnen.»

«Ich stimme dir ja zu was die Komplexität angeht.
Aber ‹wunderbar› – da bin ich mir nicht so sicher!»

«Zurück zu deinem Beispiel. Du hast gesagt, dass
Emma wahrscheinlich nicht für sehr lange in diesem
Supermarkt arbeiten wird.»

«Stimmt. Ich gebe ihr ungefähr eine Woche.»

«Deshalb könnte ihre Arbeit dort als vorübergehend
angesehen werden, oder nicht?»

«Present Continuous!»

«Das war ein kleiner logischer Sprung, aber ich denke,
du bist auf der richtigen Fährte.»

"And Jason's job at the insurance company is of a more permanent nature! So I should use, in fact I did use, the simple present!"

"Well done."

"Is that it?"

"Well, you have the very basics, there is much more to learn."

"Such as?"

"Well, for example there are some verbs which we rarely use in the continuous form."

"Such as?"

"Would you say, 'I love pop tarts' or 'I am loving pop tarts'?"

"I love pop tarts! Strawberry is my favourite."

"What about 'I am loving pop tarts'?"

"No. Because my love for pop tarts is of a very permanent nature. I will love pop tarts until the end of time!"

"Can you think of anything that you could love but only for a short time?"

"Well … But that wouldn't be love, would it?"

"No, I doubt it. There are rare cases of using the verb 'to love' in the continuous form."

"Such as?"

"How long have you been on this course?"

"Two days now."

"And what do you think of it so far?"

«Und Jasons Anstellung bei der Versicherung ist langfristiger. Und daher sollte ich das Simple Present verwenden.»

«Gut gemacht.»

«Ist das alles?»

«Nun, die Grundzüge hast du verstanden, aber du hast noch einiges vor dir.»

«Und das wäre?»

«Zum Beispiel, dass es Verben gibt, die man selten in der Continuous-Form verwendet.»

«Und welche sind das?»

«Würdest du sagen ‹I love pop tarts› oder ‹I am loving pop tarts›?»

«I love pop tarts! Und die mit Erdbeeren mag ich am liebsten.»

«Was ist mit ‹I am loving pop tarts›?»

«Nein, nein, meine Liebe für Pop-Tarts ist ungebrochen. Und das wird sich auch bestimmt niemals ändern!»

«Kannst du dir etwas vorstellen, das du vielleicht nur für eine kurze Zeit lieben könntest?»

«Na ja, das würde man dann aber nicht Liebe nennen, oder?»

«Nein, wahrscheinlich nicht. Es gibt nur ein paar wenige Fälle, in denen das Verb ‹to love› in der Continuous-Form verwendet werden kann.»

«Und das wären?»

«Wie lange bist du nun schon in diesem Kurs?»

«Zwei Tage.»

«Und was hältst du bisher von ihm?»

"RUBBISH! No, honestly, I'm loving every minute of it. Ha! I used it!"

"Indeed you did. Now, what's the capital of Canada?"

"I know! I know! It's Ottawa!"

"Well done. Most people think it's either Montreal or Toronto."

"Ha! I'm not as stupid as I look!"

"Okay, but why did you say, 'I know!', instead of, 'I am knowing'?"

"I'm not sure."

"Did you know the capital of Canada yesterday?"

"I sure did."

"And will you know it tomorrow?"

"Unless I am struck down by a bout of Alzheimer's."

"So there is an element of permanency about knowledge."

"So I have to use the simple present!"

"Correct. There are quite a few verbs like 'know' and 'love', that are not normally used in the present continuous. Think of 'have', 'hate' and 'understand', verbs that express possession, feelings or states."

"I think I'm getting the hang of this. Can I produce a little table to help my understanding of these two forms?"

"Be my guest!"

« Plunder ! Nein ehrlich, ich liebe jede einzelne Minute. Haha ! Ich hab die Continuous-Form verwendet ! »

« Das hast du ! Nun, wie heißt die Hauptstadt von Kanada ? »

« Ich weiß es, ich weiß es. Das ist Ottawa ! »

« Sehr gut. Die meisten Leute denken dabei an Montreal oder Toronto. »

« Haha ! Ich bin nicht so dumm, wie ich aussehe. »

« Okay. Aber warum hast du hier ‹ I know › genommen anstatt ‹ I am knowing › ? »

« Ich bin mir nicht sicher. »

« Wusstest du gestern, wie die Hauptstadt von Kanada heißt ? »

« Klar doch. »

« Und wirst du das morgen auch noch wissen ? »

« Ja, natürlich, es sei denn, ich bekomme auf einen Schlag Alzheimer. »

« Das heißt also, dass Wissen etwas Beständiges ist. »

« Deshalb verwende ich das Simple Present ! »

« Richtig. Es gibt noch ein paar ähnliche Verben wie ‹ know › und ‹ love ›, die normalerweise nicht im Present Continuous verwendet werden. Etwa ‹ have ›, ‹ hate › und ‹ understand ›, also Verben, die Besitz, Gefühle oder einen Zustand ausdrücken. »

« So langsam habe ich den Bogen raus. Kann ich eine kleine Tabelle machen, die mir hilft, diese beiden Formen zu verstehen ? »

« Ja, gerne. »

"Like it?"

"It's treeeemendous!"

"I don't believe you said that."

"Learning is a two-way process. You can pick up a lot from your students."

"I'll try to remember that, yet more words of wisdom ..."

"Are you now familiar with the difference between the simple present and the present continuous?"

"I think so. I'll paste that table next to my bedside table so that I can get it into my brain."

"Good work, Barry. We're getting there. Slowly but surely."

	SIMPLE PRESENT	PRESENT CONTINUOUS
FORM	The earth goes around the sun.	Emma is working in a supermarket.
FRAGE-FORM	What do lions eat?	Are you reading a good book at the moment?
VERWEN-DUNG	für sich wiederholende Handlungen oder allgemeine Aussagen, also solche, die regelmäßig, immer, jeden Tag oder nie geschehen	für Handlungen, die nur vorübergehend oder im Moment des Sprechens stattfinden
PROBLEME	wird oft mit dem Present Continuous verwechselt	wird oft mit dem Simple Present verwechselt

« Gefällt dir die Tabelle? »

« Sie ist umwerfend! »

« Fast zu schön, um wahr zu sein. »

« Lernen ist ein wechselseitiger Prozess. Man kann viel von seinen Schülern lernen. »

« Ich versuche, das im Kopf zu behalten. Noch mehr goldene Worte … »

« Verstehst du nun den Unterschied zwischen Simple Present und Present Continuous? »

« Ich denke schon. Ich lege mir die Tabelle unters Kopfkissen, so dass ich sie leichter verinnerlichen kann. »

« Gute Arbeit, Barry. Wir schaffen das schon. Langsam, aber sicher. »

Perfect Present – Present Perfect!

"I've been looking at your C. V. (curriculum vitae), Barry."

"What do you reckon? Will employers be begging me to work for them?"

"It depends how desperate they are."

"Gee, thanks. You're supposed to be helping me get a job!"

"I'm trying my best, honestly. Anyway, you've had two jobs so far in your life."

"That's true. Shelf stacker at Poundland …"

"Are you still working as a shelf stacker in Poundland?"

"No way! The wages were terrible and my boss was horrible!"

"So when did you finish your work at Pound-land?"

Perfect Present – Present Perfect!

«Ich habe mir deinen Lebenslauf angesehen, Barry.»

«Und was denkst du? Werden sich die Arbeitgeber die Finger nach mir lecken?»

«Das hängt davon ab, wie verzweifelt ihre Lage ist.»

«Na sauber, danke dir. Du sollst mir doch helfen, eine Anstellung zu bekommen!»

«Ich tue mein Bestes, ehrlich! Hattest du nicht schon zwei Stellen?»

«Stimmt. Regaleinräumer bei der Firma Poundland ...»

«Arbeitest du immer noch als Regaleinräumer bei dieser Firma?»

«Auf keinen Fall! Mein Lohn war miserabel und der Chef schrecklich!»

«Wann hast du mit der Arbeit bei Poundland aufgehört?»

"October last year."

"In the past."

"Definitely."

"You don't work there any more."

"Listen, cloth ears – I don't work in Pound-land any more. It's over. Finished."

"Cloth ears, I don't think you've called me that before."

"Well you don't seem to be listening. I don't work in Poundland any more. And before you ask, I don't work in the King's Head any more either."

"What work did you do in the King's Head?"

"I collected glasses and put them in the dish-washer."

"How long did you work there?"

"Three weeks."

"But you don't work there any more."

"You know that already !"

"I do, but I'm just asking some checking ques-tions."

"Did you pack this bag yourself? Has anyone given you anything to take on this flight? Do you have any of these items in your hand lug-gage?"

"Check*ing* questions, not check-*in* questions."

"I know that – I'm not stupid. I just hope the Germans will appreciate my razor sharp wit."

"Hmm, remind me again, how many jobs have you had in your life so far?"

«Letztes Jahr im Oktober.»

«In der Vergangenheit also.»

«Hundertpro.»

«Du arbeitest also nicht mehr dort?»

«Hör doch mal zu, du Dödel. Ich arbeite nicht mehr bei Poundland. Fertig.»

«Dödel? So hast du mich ja noch nie genannt.»

«Du hörst einfach nicht zu. Ich arbeite nicht mehr bei Poundland. Und bevor du fragst: Ich arbeite auch nicht mehr im King's Head.»

«Was hast du im King's Head gemacht?»

«Gläser eingesammelt und in die Spülmaschine gestellt.»

«Wie lange hast du dort gearbeitet?»

«Drei Wochen lang.»

«Du arbeitest also nicht mehr dort.»

«Das weißt du doch schon!»

«Das stimmt. Ich stelle nur ein paar Kontrollfragen.»

«Haben Sie die Tasche selbst gepackt? Hat Ihnen jemand etwas auf diesen Flug mitgegeben? Haben Sie eines dieser Dinge in Ihrem Handgepäck?»

«Checking-Fragen, nicht Check-in-Fragen.»

«Ich weiß. Dumm bin ich nicht. Ich hoffe nur, dass meine deutschen Schüler meinen messerscharfen Witz verstehen.»

«Okay, wie viele Jobs hast du gleich nochmal gehabt?»

"Two."

"And do you think that it is realistic that you might have another job in the future?"

"I definitely hope so!"

"Okay, now let's look at something else. Where do you live?"

"In a flat above the chip shop."

"When did you move into that flat?"

"Six months ago."

"In the past."

"Great work, Sherlock."

"And you still live there?"

"Yeah, it's great. I get ten per cent off my fish and chips!"

"Now, I'm trying to work something out. You moved in six months ago and you still live there. That means …"

"*I've lived* in the flat above the chip shop for six months!"

"Excellent!"

"It's a bit of a dump actually but it's cheap."

"I was referring to your use of grammar."

"What grammar was that?"

"*The present perfect!*"

"Never heard of it."

"Now why am I not surprised? It is a very common tense."

"So what bit was the perfect present?"

"*The present perfect,* although you'd rather have pop tarts as a present. You told me about

«Zwei.»

«Und ist es wahrscheinlich, dass du einen neuen Job bekommst?»

«Das hoffe ich doch!»

«Gut. Wenden wir uns etwas anderem zu. Wo wohnst du?»

«In einer Wohnung über einer Frittenbude.»

«Wann bist du in diese Wohnung eingezogen?»

«Vor sechs Monaten.»

«In der Vergangenheit also.»

«Gute Arbeit, Sherlock!»

«Wohnst du noch dort?»

«Ja, da gefällt es mir. Ich bekomme zehn Prozent Rabatt auf meine Fish & Chips.»

«Nun will ich mal etwas ausprobieren. Du bist vor sechs Monaten eingezogen und wohnst immer noch da. Das bedeutet …»

«Ich wohne seit sechs Monaten in der Wohnung über der Frittenbude.»

«Ausgezeichnet!»

«Na ja, es ist zwar ein Loch, aber dafür billig.»

«Ich habe die verwendete Grammatik gemeint.»

«Welche meinst du?»

«Das Present Perfect!»

«Davon habe ich noch nie gehört.»

«Was mich nicht überrascht! Es ist eine sehr gebräuchliche Zeitform.»

«Und was war das für ein Perfect Present?»

«Das Present Perfect, auch wenn du wohl lieber Pop-Tarts geschenkt bekommen würdest. Du hast mir von

an event which began in the past and continues up to the present."

"I did?"

"Yes, about living in the flat above the chip shop."

"*I have lived* in the flat above the chip shop for six months."

"Exactly. A great example. An event which began in the past and continues up to the present."

"Wait a minute, earlier you asked me about my jobs."

"That's true."

"You said, '*you've had* two jobs'. But that, according to your grammar rule, is wrong."

"I don't think you will ever know how much that hurts."

"But you said the *present perfect* is an event which began in the past and continues up to the present."

"Correct."

"But I don't work in Poundland or the King's Head any more. Those events are both in the past. They don't continue up to the present. You are … could you explain the error in my thinking which I am clearly unable to see?"

"Ah, that's better, Barry. Now, I remember saying '*you've had* two jobs so far in your life'."

"Yes, I remember that. But, but, they're over. Finished …"

einem Ereignis erzählt, das in der Vergangenheit begonnen hat und bis in die Gegenwart dauert. »

« Hab ich? »

« Ja, darüber, dass du in einer Wohnung über einer Frittenbude wohnst. »

« Ich wohne seit sechs Monaten in der Wohnung über der Frittenbude. »

« Genau. Das ist ein sehr gutes Beispiel. Ein Ereignis, das in der Vergangenheit begann und bis in die Gegenwart andauert. »

« Warte mal, du hast mich vorher nach meinen Jobs gefragt. »

« Stimmt. »

« Du hast ‹ yo've had two jobs › gesagt. Aber deiner Grammatikregel nach ist das falsch. »

« Ich glaube nicht, dass du jemals merkst, wie weh das tut. »

« Aber du hast gesagt, das Present Perfect beschreibt ein Ereignis, das in der Vergangenheit begann und bis in die Gegenwart andauert. »

« Richtig. »

« Aber ich arbeite nun weder bei Poundland noch im King's Head. Beide Ereignisse liegen in der Vergangenheit. Sie dauern nicht bis in die Gegenwart. Du bist … Oder sehe ich das ganz falsch? Kannst du mir das erklären? »

« Gut, das ist besser, Barry. Nun, ich erinnere mich daran ‹ you've had two jobs so far in your life › gesagt zu haben. »

« Ja, das weiß ich. Aber das ist vorbei. Abgeschlossen … »

"True, those jobs are over, but what about your life?"

"That hasn't finished yet."

"Exactly!"

"Okay, but why is this important in the perfect present?"

"*The present perfect!* Because we are looking at a time period which continues up to the present. You are still alive. There is a chance that you might have another job in the future."

"You sure?"

"It's definitely possible. Now, you might not know this, but Albert Einstein worked in Poundland as a shelf stacker."

"He did?"

"Hundred per cent. Before working at Princeton he spent six months stacking shelves in Poundland."

«Sicher, die Jobs sind Vergangenheit, aber was ist mit deinem Leben?»

«Das ist noch nicht zu Ende.»

«Richtig!»

«Gut, aber warum ist das beim Perfect Present so wichtig?»

«Beim Present Perfect! Weil wir einen Zeitpunkt betrachten, der bis in die Gegenwart reicht. Du lebst immer noch. Es besteht durchaus die Möglichkeit, dass du in der Zukunft einen neuen Job findest.»

«Bist du sicher?»

«Es ist absolut möglich. Nun, du wirst es vielleicht nicht wissen, aber Albert Einstein hat bei Poundland als Regalauffüller gearbeitet.»

«Wirklich?»

«Ohne Zweifel. Bevor er an der Uni Princeton angefangen hat, hat er sechs Monate lang bei Poundland Regale eingeräumt.»

"Wow, I would never have thought that."

"Not a lot of people would. Anyway, shelf stacker at Poundland and Professor at Princeton : two jobs."

"Wow, just like me !"

"What do you mean?"

"Well, Einstein had two jobs and *I've had* two jobs ! The coincidence is uncanny."

"Very interesting. What did you say about Einstein?"

"He *had* two jobs."

"And what did you say about yourself?"

"*I've had* two jobs."

"You used different tenses for you and for Einstein."

"I did?"

"You definitely did – and it was correct. But most importantly, why was there a difference? What is the difference between Albert Einstein and you?"

"About a hundred IQ points?"

"Yes, and …?"

"Er, he's dead?"

"Exactly ! Mr Einstein had two jobs. There is no way he is going to have any more jobs in the future."

"Whereas I am still alive and, with a bit of luck, I might have some more jobs in the future."

"Wow, Barry, I think we're getting there."

"It's not that difficult really."

«Wow, das hätte ich nie gedacht.»

«Nicht viele Leute wissen das. Egal, Regalauffüller bei Poundland und Professor an der Uni Princeton – das sind zwei Tätigkeiten.»

«Wow, genau wie ich!»

«Was meinst du damit?»

«Nun, Einstein hatte zwei Jobs, und ich habe auch zwei gehabt! Der Zufall ist fast unheimlich.»

«Wirklich interessant. Was hast du über Einstein gesagt?»

«Er hatte zwei Jobs.»

«Und was hast du über dich erzählt?»

«Ich habe zwei Jobs gehabt.»

«Du hast für dich und Einstein zwei unterschiedliche Zeitformen verwendet.»

«Hab ich?»

«Absolut, und richtig war es auch. Aber noch wichtiger ist, warum da ein Unterschied besteht. Worin unterscheiden sich Einstein und du?»

«In ungefähr hundert IQ-Punkten?»

«Ja, und …?»

«Hm, dass er tot ist?»

«Genau! Herr Einstein hatte zwei Tätigkeiten, und es ist ziemlich ausgeschlossen, dass er in der Zukunft je wieder eine haben wird.»

«Während ich noch lebe und mit ein wenig Glück in der Zukunft noch ein paar Jobs haben könnte.»

«Nicht schlecht, Barry. Allmählich wird es.»

«Ist eigentlich auch gar nicht so schwierig.»

"It isn't for you as *you've grown* up with it but it is a big problem for Germans."

"What, even Einstein?"

"I'm not sure how good he was with the present perfect but it is pretty common for Germans to say, 'Last year we have visited Scotland'."

"That's wrong!"

"Can you explain why?"

"Easy. Last year *I visited* Torremolinos in Spain, not Scotland."

"Okay, but what is wrong with the grammar?"

"Well I'm not in Torremolinos any more so I have to use the past simple, I visited."

"Correct! How many times *have you visited* Torremolinos?"

"*I have visited* Torremolinos four times."

"Can you explain the grammar there?"

"Yes! I'm still alive! I'm definitely going to visit Torremolinos again in the future."

"Lucky you."

"Yes, and unlucky Mr Einstein. He never visited Torremolinos. In fact he's never going to visit Torremolinos – because he's not alive like me!"

"I think you're getting there."

"I think am. But why do the Germans say 'Last year we have visited Scotland'? You explained the grammar to me in ten minutes. Why can't they get it? Are they … a bit slow?"

«Für dich nicht, da du damit aufgewachsen bist; aber für Deutsche, die Englisch lernen, ist es ein großes Problem.»

«Was, auch für Einstein?»

«Ich bin nicht sicher, wie gut er mit dem Present Perfect zurechtkam, aber viele Deutsche sagen: ‹Last year we have visited Scotland.›»

«Das ist aber falsch!»

«Kannst du erklären, warum?»

«Das ist einfach. Letztes Jahr war ich in Torremolinos in Spanien, nicht in Schottland.»

«Gut, aber was stimmt mit der Grammatik nicht?»

«Nun, ich bin jetzt nicht mehr in Torremolinos. Deshalb habe ich die einfache Vergangenheit benutzt, das Simple Past.»

«Richtig! Wie oft bist du schon in Torremolinos gewesen?»

«Ich bin bereits viermal in Torremolinos gewesen.»

«Kannst du mir hier die Grammatik erklären?»

«Ja! Ich lebe noch! Und ich werde sicher nochmals nach Torremolinos fahren.»

«Du Glückspilz.»

«Ja, und Pech für Herrn Einstein. Er war nie in Torremolinos. Und wird auch niemals nach Torremolinos reisen – da er im Gegensatz zu mir nicht mehr am Leben ist!»

«So langsam verstehst du das, oder?»

«Ich denke, schon. Aber warum sagen die Deutschen: ‹Last year we have visited Scotland›? Du hast mir die Grammatik in zehn Minuten erklärt. Warum verstehen sie das nicht? Sind sie vielleicht ein bisschen … langsam?»

"Because it is a direct translation from German – and if a German explained the second conjunctive or the genitive case to you in ten minutes, do you think you'd get it straight away?"

"I had conjunctivitis once, I had horrible red eyes and my mum had to squeeze this white cream onto my eyeballs and ... sorry, what is the second conjunctive when it's at home?"

"Ah, just one of the delights that await you when you learn German."

"I don't need a genitive case. My mum bought me a really nice Samsonite case for my birthday."

"Ah, you have so much to learn, Barry. Now the reasons that Germans have problems with the *present perfect* is that in German they use the present perfect and the simple past in the same way. 'Ich habe gegessen' means 'I ate' but so does 'ich aß'."

"Ha ha!"

"What's so funny?"

"You just said 'ass'."

"Explain that to the Germans and they'll split their sides laughing."

"Really?"

"No. Now, have you got the *present perfect*? In particular the difference between the present perfect and the simple past."

"Sure I have. I'll make a little table to prove it."

«Weil es die wörtliche Übersetzung des deutschen Satzes ist. Und wenn dir ein Deutscher den Konjunktiv II oder den Genitiv in gerade einmal zehn Minuten erklären würde, würdest du das dann gleich kapieren?»

«Ich hatte schon mal Konjunktivitis. Ich hatte schrecklich rote Augen, und meine Mutter musste eine weiße Salbe auf meine Augäpfel schmieren und … Entschuldigung, was ist der Konjunktiv II? Aber bitte so, dass ich es auch verstehe.»

«Oh, nur eine der Freuden, die dich erwarten, wenn du Deutsch lernst.»

«Einen ‹Genitiv› brauche ich aber nicht. Meine Mutter hat mir einen wirklich schönen ‹Samsonite› zum Geburtstag geschenkt.»

«Oje, du musst noch so viel lernen. Der Grund, weshalb viele Deutsche Probleme mit dem Present Perfect haben, liegt darin, dass im Deutschen das Present Perfect und das Simple Past in der Umgangssprache unterschiedslos verwendet werden. ‹Ich habe gegessen› oder ‹ich aß›!»

«Haha!»

«Was ist so lustig?»

«Du hast gerade ‹ich Arsch› gesagt.»

«Erklär das mal deinen deutschen Schülern, die werden sich totlachen.»

«Wirklich?»

«Nein. Hast du das Present Perfect nun verstanden? Besonders den Unterschied zwischen Present Perfect und Simple Past.»

«Klar! Ich mach eine kleine Tabelle, dann siehst du's.»

"Like it?"

"I love it, Barry. I don't think I could have done a better job myself."

"I'll print it out and give it to someone in Germany."

"I'm sure they'll appreciate it."

"Yes, gift-wrapped – it'll be the perfect present!"

"Ow!"

"What's wrong?"

"I cut myself."

"On what?"

"On your razor-sharp wit."

	VERWENDUNG	BEISPIEL
Present Perfect	um Ereignisse zu beschreiben, die in der Vergangenheit begannen und bis in die Gegenwart andauern	I have visited Scotland sixty-five times (and I'm still alive and I might go again).
Simple Past	um Handlungen zu beschreiben, die in der Vergangenheit abgeschlossen sind. Es steht meistens eine Zeitangabe (yesterday, last year …) dabei	Albert Einstein visited Scotland three times (and he's dead so he'll never go again).

«Gefällt sie dir?»

«Wirklich großartig, Barry. Ich denke nicht, dass ich es hätte besser machen können.»

«Ich drucke die Tabelle aus und gebe sie in Deutschland weiter.»

«Ich bin sicher, man wird es dort zu schätzen wissen.»

«Ja, als Geschenk eingepackt – das perfekte Präsent!»

«Autsch!»

«Ist was passiert?»

«Ich habe mich geschnitten.»

«Woran?»

«An deinem rasiermesserscharfen Witz.»

Hair Conditionals

"Come on, Barry, you're late for class!"

"I'm sorry. I had to call my mother."

"Well, *if you hadn't called* your mother, *you would have got* here on time."

"Yes, but you don't know my mother. *If I didn't call* her once a week, *she would kill* me. Don't you ever call your mother?"

"*If I have time,* then *I call her,* but I have to admit, that isn't very often."

"*If you want* to, *you can go and call* her right now."

"No, no. *If I call* her from work, *she'll think* that something has happened to me."

"I have to say your hair looks lovely."

"Thank you. I used some new conditioner. *If you want* to, *you can borrow* it."

"Have you noticed something?"

Haarige Conditionals

«Los, komm, Barry, du bist spät dran!»

«Tut mir leid. Ich musste noch meine Mutter anrufen.»

«Nun, wenn du nicht deine Mutter angerufen hättest, dann wärst du rechtzeitig zum Unterricht gekommen.»

«Ja, aber du kennst meine Mutter nicht. Wenn ich sie nicht einmal in der Woche anriefe, würde sie mich umbringen. Rufst du deine Mutter niemals an?»

«Wenn ich Zeit habe, rufe ich sie an. Aber ich gebe zu, das ist nicht sehr oft.»

«Wenn du möchtest, kannst du sie gerne jetzt anrufen.»

«Nein, nein. Wenn ich sie von der Arbeit aus anrufe, dann wird sie denken, dass mir etwas passiert ist.»

«Übrigens, ich muss sagen, dein Haar sieht gut aus.»

«Danke. Ich habe einen neuen Conditioner verwendet. Wenn du willst, kannst du ihn gerne ausleihen.»

«Ist dir etwas aufgefallen?»

"What would that be?"

"There were an amazing numbers of '*ifs*' in our opening dialogue."

"Really? How convenient. It might help us in our lesson today. Now, Barry. Are you any good at science?"

"Well, I did a bit at school."

"Perfect. Okay, I have a question."

"Ooooh, a quiz! I love quizzes, me."

"Yes, well ... Okay, first question. If I heat water to a hundred degrees Celsius. What happens to it?"

"That one's easy. It boils!"

"Correct. Second question. If plants get only electric light, not sunlight, what happens to them?"

"I know! I know! They die!"

"Right again. You're not as stupid as you look!"

"Hey, thanks. Third question please!"

"If iron is left out in the rain, what happens to it?"

"It rusts!"

"Can you be a little more scientific?"

"It oxidizes!"

"Four syllables – and it was the correct answer. Well done."

"Hey, I thought you were training me to be an English teacher. Surely we shouldn't be messing around with quizzes, however fun they are."

«Was soll mir aufgefallen sein?»

«Wir haben in unserem Gespräch gerade eine unglaublich große Anzahl ‹ifs› verwendet.»

«Wirklich? Wie passend. Das fügt sich gut in unsere Unterrichtsstunde. Und nun, Barry, bist du naturwissenschaftlich gut drauf?»

«Na, ich hatte die Fächer in der Schule.»

«Wunderbar. Nun eine Frage.»

«Oh, ein neues Frage-und-Antwort-Spiel! Super.»

«Na ja … Gut, hier also die erste Frage: Was passiert, wenn man Wasser auf hundert Grad Celsius erhitzt?»

«Das ist aber einfach. Es kocht.»

«Richtig. Frage zwei: Wenn Pflanzen kein Sonnenlicht, sondern nur elektrisches Licht bekommen, was geschieht dann?»

«Ich weiß, ich weiß, dann sterben sie!»

«Stimmt schon wieder. Du bist nicht so dumm, wie du aussiehst.»

«Hallo? Die dritte Frage bitte.»

«Wenn Eisen nass wird, was passiert dann?»

«Es rostet!»

«Geht's auch etwas wissenschaftlicher?»

«Es oxidiert!»

«Wow, drei Silben, und es war zudem die richtige Antwort. Gut gemacht.»

«Hallo? Ich dachte, du wolltest aus mir einen guten Englischlehrer machen. Wir sollten wohl nicht die Zeit mit Frage-und-Antwort-Spielen vertun, auch wenn sie lustig sind.»

"There is method in my madness, oh stupid one."

"I guess I'll have to wait and find out what it is."

"No you won't. We've already done the first one."

"Done one what? Quiz?"

"Conditional form. We looked at the *zero conditional*."

"The what?"

"The *zero conditional*. We often use this when we talk about cause and effect. If X happens, Y is the result."

"What, you mean like in the quiz: *If I heat water to a hundred degrees Celsius, it boils!*"

"Exactly. I recommend you use that sentence as a model sentence."

"Good idea."

"Okay, now in your model sentence. *If I heat water to a hundred degrees Celsius, it boils!* Are we talking about a particular kettle or saucepan full of water?"

"No. We're talking about water in general, nothing specific."

"Right. That's an important part of the *zero conditional*. Not a specific time or place."

"If I call my sister a wally, she thumps me."

"Excellent!"

"No it's not. It bloody hurts!"

« Meine Methode hat System, du Dumm-
kopf. »

« Ich denke, ich muss das noch herausfinden. »

« Nein, brauchst du nicht. Den ersten Schritt haben
wir schon getan. »

« Was getan? Ein Frage-und-Antwort-Spiel gespielt? »

« Nein, das Conditional verwendet. Wir haben uns
gerade mit dem Zero Conditional beschäftigt. »

« Mit dem was? »

« Dem Zero Conditional. Wir verwenden das häufig,
um über Ursache und Wirkung zu sprechen. Wenn x
passiert, so führt das zu y. »

« Meinst du etwa so wie im Frage-und-Antwort-Spiel :
Wenn man Wasser auf hundert Grad Celsius erhitzt,
dann kocht es? »

« Genau. Ich würde vorschlagen, dass du dir diesen
Satz als Beispielsatz merkst. »

« Gute Idee. »

« Schauen wir uns den Satz nochmal an : Wenn man
Wasser auf hundert Grad Celsius erhitzt, dann kocht es !
Sprechen wir über einen bestimmten Wasserkocher oder
einen Topf mit Wasser? »

« Keines von beiden. Wir sprechen über Wasser allgemein. Nichts Spezifisches. »

« Richtig. Das ist ein Kennzeichen des Zero Conditional.
Weder eine spezifische Zeit noch ein spezifischer Ort. »

« Wenn ich meine Schwester ‹ Trottel › nenne, dann
schlägt sie mich. »

« Klasse ! »

« Nein, ist es gar nicht. Es tut teuflisch weh ! »

"But a good example of the zero conditional. Just checking, I presume it is a fairly common or likely event?"

"Daily."

"Poor guy ! But it's time to move on. Now, I've just moved into a new house. There is a garden at the back and frankly I'm a useless gardener. Could you give me some tips?"

"Sure, I've got some flowers in my back garden. What's your problem?"

"Well, I've got some marvellous marigolds, some dazzling* daisies and some beautiful buttercups …"

"Amazing alliteration, oh great master."

"Thank you. Anyway. I have been given conflicting advice by my neighbours and frankly, I'm at a loss as to what to do."

---

* dazzling: glänzend, strahlend schön

« Aber es ist ein gutes Beispiel für das Zero Conditional. Nur, um mich zu vergewissern: Ich nehme an, es passiert täglich oder ist zumindest sehr wahrscheinlich. »

« Täglich. »

« Armer Kerl. Aber lass uns weitermachen. Ich bin gerade in ein neues Haus gezogen. Auf der Rückseite des Hauses gibt es einen Garten. Aber ganz offen gesagt, ich bin ein ziemlich schlechter Gärtner. Hättest du ein paar Tipps für mich? »

« Klar doch. Ich habe ein paar Blumen in meinem Garten. Was ist dein Problem? »

« Nun, ich habe ein paar riesengroße Ringelblumen, einige grazile Gänseblümchen und ein paar blassgelbe Butterblumen … »*

« Eine ausgezeichnete Alliteration, großer Meister. »

« Danke dir. Ich habe von meinen Nachbarn so unterschiedliche Ratschläge bekommen, dass ich wirklich nicht mehr weiß, was ich tun soll. »

---

* Um die Alliteration wiederzugeben, werden hier abweichende Adjektive verwendet.

FIRST

"So what did they tell you?"

"Mr Aardvark told me to put manure around my flowers. Mr Baboon told me to give them all a good dose of cyanide. Mr Cabbage suggested that I pour concrete over my whole garden. Now what do you think? You're the expert."

"Well, Mr Aardvark clearly knows what he's talking about. If you put manure around your flowers, they will grow twice as fast."

"Really? My marigolds, my daisies and my buttercups?"

"Yes, your flowers. But Mr Baboon's cyanide is a really bad idea."

"Really?"

"Yes. If you put cyanide on your flowers, they'll all be dead in a couple of days."

"You mean the flowers in my back garden, those specific flowers."

"Yes, those specific flowers."

"Just checking."

"As for Mr Cabbage, well, I don't know where he studied gardening! He should definitely ask for his money back! If you pour concrete over your flowers, they will die!"

"Die?!"

"Yes, if you cover them with concrete, they won't be able to get the sunlight they need."

« Was haben sie dir denn gesagt? »

« Mr Aardvark meinte, ich solle Dünger um meine Blumen herum verteilen. Mr Baboon sagte, ich solle ihnen eine gute Dosis Zyanid verabreichen. Und Mr Cabbage schlug vor, meinen ganzen Garten mit Beton zu bedecken. Was denkst du? Du bist der Experte. »

« Mr Aardvark kennt sich aus. Wenn du deine Blumen düngst, dann werden sie doppelt so schnell wachsen. »

« Wirklich? Meine Ringelblumen, Gänseblümchen und Butterblumen? »

« Ja, deine Blumen. Aber Mr Baboons Idee mit dem Zyanid ist ziemlich schlecht. »

« Wirklich? »

« Ja, wenn du Zyanid auf deine Blumen gibst, dann werden sie innerhalb von ein paar Tagen tot sein. »

« Du meinst die Blumen in meinen Garten, die und keine anderen. »

« Ja, diese speziellen Blumen. »

« Wollte mich nur vergewissern. »

« Und was Mr Cabbage angeht – ich weiß wirklich nicht, wo der das Gärtnerhandwerk gelernt hat! Er sollte wirklich sein Geld zurückverlangen! Wenn du Beton über deine Blumen gießt, werden sie sterben! »

« Sterben?! »

« Ja, wenn du die Blumen mit Beton bedeckst, werden sie das benötigte Sonnenlicht nicht bekommen. »

"Wow, Barry, you're a real green-fingered expert!"

"Yes, well, once again you've led me astray."

"Not at all."

"What do you mean, not at all? I'm here to learn how English grammar works and instead of teaching me, you pick my brain for gardening tips!"

"There is method in my madness ..."

"... oh stupid one. Ha ha. I was hoping there might be."

"We were talking about my options for the future."

"The options for your marvellous marigolds and ... the others."

"Exactly. We are looking at possible situations in the future, but with an element of conditionality about them."

"You mean, there's an 'if' in the sentence."

"Often, but not always. But our model sentence, fortunately, has one."

"So which one is our model sentence?"

"You can choose!"

"Well, Mr Aardvark gave the most sensible advice, but I don't find sensible things easy to remember."

"Really?"

"Yes. So my model sentence will be: *If you pour concrete over your flowers, they will die!* Now what was this form called?"

«Wow, Barry, du hast wohl wirklich einen grünen Daumen!»

«Ja, und du hast mich schon wieder irregeführt.»

«Nein, überhaupt nicht.»

«Was meinst du mit ‹überhaupt nicht›? Ich bin hier, um zu lernen, wie die englische Grammatik funktioniert, und anstatt dass du mir das beibringst, soll ich dir mit Pflanzentipps kommen!»

«Meine Methode hat System ...»

«... du Witzbold. Haha. Ich hatte gehofft, dass dem so wäre.»

«Wir haben über meine zukünftigen Möglichkeiten geredet.»

«Die Aussichten für deine riesengroßen Ringelblumen und die anderen ...»

«Genau. Wir schauen uns ein paar mögliche Gegebenheiten in der Zukunft an, die aber alle auf einer bedingten Annahme beruhen.»

«Meinst du Sätze mit einem ‹if›?»

«Oft, aber nicht immer. Aber unser Beispielsatz hat zum Glück eines.»

«Welcher Beispielsatz?»

«Du kannst wählen!»

«Mr Aardvark gab den vernünftigsten Rat. Das Problem ist nur, dass ich gute Ratschläge schlecht behalten kann.»

«Wirklich?»

«Ja. Mein Beispielsatz heißt also: Wenn du Beton über deine Blumen gießt, dann werden sie sterben! Nun, wie heißt diese Zeitform?»

"This is the *First conditional*."

"*First conditional*. I must write that down. *If I don't write* it down, *I'll forget* it!"

"Excellent. You've definitely got the hang of this one pretty quickly. So, what are your plans for this afternoon?"

"I'm not sure. It depends on the weather. I might go swimming in the sea."

"Only might?"

"It depends on the weather."

"You mean, that you want to go swimming, but only on the condition that the weather is good."

"Correct. *If it's sunny, I'll go swimming*. If it's pi…ouring with rain, I'll stay at home and study English grammar."

"Perfect. Can I just point out something interesting?"

"If you want to."

"If it's sunny …"

"Is that interesting?"

"You are talking about this afternoon, but you don't use 'will' in that part of the sentence."

"If it will be sunny …? But that sounds pretty stupid."

"To you it might sound stupid but it sounds perfectly natural to the millions of learners of ·English."

"The Great Unwashed!"

"Hey, don't forget who's going to be paying your future salary!"

« Das ist das First Conditional. »

« First Conditional. Das muss ich aufschreiben. Wenn ich es nicht aufschreibe, dann werde ich es vergessen. »

« Ausgezeichnet. Das hast du ziemlich schnell verstanden. Jetzt aber, was sind deine Pläne für heute Nachmittag? »

« Ich weiß noch nicht genau. Das hängt ganz vom Wetter ab. Kann sein, ich geh zum Schwimmen ans Meer. »

« Nur ‹ kann sein ›? »

« Es hängt vom Wetter ab. »

« Du meinst, du willst schwimmen gehen, gehst aber nur, wenn das Wetter gut ist? »

« Richtig. Wenn die Sonne scheint, werde ich schwimmen gehen. Falls es pi … regnet, werde ich zuhause bleiben und mich der englischen Grammatik widmen. »

« Perfekt. Darf ich dich kurz auf etwas Interessantes aufmerksam machen? »

« Wenn du willst. »

« Wenn die Sonne scheint … »

« Ist das interessant? »

« Du beziehst dich auf den Nachmittag, aber du benutzt in diesem Satz kein ‹ will ›, also kein Futur. »

« ‹ Wenn die Sonne scheinen wird … ›, das hört sich ziemlich blöd an. »

« Für dich mag es sich blöd anhören, aber es klingt vollkommen natürlich für die vielen Millionen Menschen, die Englisch lernen. »

« Pöbel ! »

« He, pass auf ! Denk immer daran, wer dein zukünftiges Gehalt zahlen wird. »

"Ah yes. The wonderful German public. A case of 'Don't bite the hand that feeds you!'"

"Exactly. *If you bite* the hand that feeds you, *it won't feed* you anymore."

"All right, I take your point. I'll treat my pupils with greater respect in future. Can we move on?"

"Sure, but before we do, I think you should make a table showing the two structures we have looked at so far."

"Okay, *If you want* me to, *I'll have* a go."

"So, what do you think?"

"I'm lost for words, Barry. I couldn't have done a better one myself."

"But you didn't even try!"

"True, but, anyway. We've got to move on. Are you familiar with the term 'Doppelganger'?"

"Sure!"

"You are?"

«Stimmt. Meine wunderbaren deutschen Schüler. Also im Sinne von ‹Man soll nicht die Hand beißen, die einen füttert!›»

«Genau! Wenn du die Hand beißt, die dich füttert, dann wird sie dich nicht mehr füttern.»

«Gut. Ich verstehe, was du meinst. Ich werde meine Schüler in Zukunft mit etwas mehr Respekt behandeln. Können wir weitermachen?»

«Klar. Aber ich denke, du solltest vorher noch eine von deinen Tabellen erstellen, mit Erklärungen und Beispielsätzen wie sonst auch.»

«Gut. Wenn du willst, werde ich das gerne einmal versuchen.»

NAME	KONSTRUK-TION	VERWEN-DUNG	BEISPIEL-SATZ
Zero Conditional	If+Present Tense + Present Tense	generelle Aussagen über die Gegenwart	If I heat water to hundred degrees Celsius, it boils.
First Conditional	If+Present Tense + Will Future	konditionelle Aussagen über die Zukunft	If you pour concrete over your flowers, they will die.

«Und, was denkst du?»

«Ich bin sprachlos, Barry. Ich hätte das nicht besser machen können.»

«Du hast es ja nicht einmal versucht!»

«Stimmt. Aber trotzdem. Lass uns weitermachen. Weißt du, was ein ‹Doppelgänger› ist?»

«Klar!»

«Sicher?»

"Yeah, I had one for lunch. A doppelganger with fries and a banana milkshake."

"Well, perhaps you did, but there is another meaning of the word 'doppelganger'. It means someone who looks like you. And I'd like to tell you that you have a doppelganger."

"Really? Who is it?"

"His name's Mr Bean …"

"Mr Bean? You mean that wally on TV?"

"Exactly! When I first saw you, I thought, I know that face. I was actually really surprised to find out that your name isn't Mr Bean."

"But I don't look anything like Mr Bean!"

"Oh you do, your hair, your teeth, your face, your voice …"

"What a load of bollards! *If I looked* like Mr Bean *I would cry* myself to sleep every night."

"But your hair …"

"*If I had* hair like Mr Bean *I would shave* it all off."

"And your teeth …"

"*If I had* teeth like Mr Bean, *I would pull* them all out."

"And your face …"

"*If I had* a face like Mr Bean's *I would ask* a cosmetic surgeon to do a lot of work."

"And your voice …"

"*If I spoke* like Mr Bean *I would go* to a speech therapist."

«Ja, und ich hatte sogar einen zum Lunch. Einen ‹Doppelgänger› mit Pommes und einen Bananenmilchshake.»

«Nun, vielleicht hattest du ja einen solchen. Aber das Wort beschreibt eigentlich jemanden, der so aussieht wie du. Und ich bin mir sicher, dass du einen Doppelgänger hast.»

«Wirklich? Und wer soll das sein?»

«Mr Bean …»

«Mr Bean? Du meinst den Blödmann aus dem Fernsehen?»

«Genau! Als ich dich zum ersten Mal sah, dachte ich, dieses Gesicht kennst du. Ich war daher ziemlich überrascht, dass du nicht Mr Bean heißt.»

«Aber ich sehe wirklich nicht aus wie Mr Bean!»

«Doch, tust du. Dein Haar, deine Zähne, dein Gesicht, deine Stimme …»

«Was für ein Blödsinn! Sähe ich wie Mr Bean aus, würde ich mich jeden Abend in den Schlaf heulen.»

«Aber deine Haare …»

«Hätte ich Haare wie Mr Bean, würde ich mir alle abrasieren.»

«Und deine Zähne …»

«Hätte ich Zähne wie Mr Bean, würde ich mir die alle ausreißen.»

«Und dein Gesicht …»

«Hätte ich das Gesicht von Mr Bean, würde ich einen Schönheitschirurgen um tatkräftige Hilfe bitten.»

«Und deine Stimme …»

«Spräche ich so wie Mr Bean, würde ich zu einem Sprachtherapeuten gehen.»

"Can I tell you something?"

"What?"

"I was only joking."

"What?!"

"I was doing a bit of subtle eliciting."

"You were?"

"I was. Now let's look at some very interesting things you said: Now, my first question is, do you, at this moment in time, look remotely like Mr Bean?"

"No!!!"

"So we are talking about something purely hypothetical, or at least, very unlikely."

"Correct."

"Okay, now let's look at your next model sentence. I referred to your, I now admit, totally untrue similarity to Mr Bean. Your reply was, and I quote: What a load of bollards! *If I looked like Mr Bean, I would cry myself to sleep every night.*"

"Too true."

"This is an example of the *second conditional.*"

"It is?"

"Yes, it is. We use the second conditional when we're talking about a situation in the present that is plainly untrue, or very unlikely."

"Okay, but *if I were you, I wouldn't tell* people that they look like Mr Bean. They could get angry and punch you on the nose."

"Are you me?"

«Soll ich dir was sagen?»

«Was?»

«Ich habe nur Spaß gemacht.»

«Was?!»

«Ich hab nur versucht, dir ein paar Dinge zu entlocken.»

«Wirklich?»

«Ja. Jetzt lass uns einmal nachsehen, was für interessante Dinge du gesagt hast. Meine erste Frage ist aber: Siehst du überhaupt im Entferntesten aus wie Mr Bean?»

«Nein!!!»

«Wir sprechen also über etwas rein Hypothetisches oder zumindest etwas sehr Unwahrscheinliches.»

«Richtig.»

«Gut. Gehen wir weiter zu deinem nächsten Beispielsatz. Ich habe mich, und ich gebe das zu, auf deine nicht existente Ähnlichkeit mit Mr Bean bezogen. Und deine Antwort war, und ich zitiere: ‹Was für ein Blödsinn! Sähe ich wie Mr Bean aus, würde ich mich jeden Abend in den Schlaf heulen!›»

«Das ist wahr.»

«Das ist ein Beispiel für das Second Conditional.»

«Wirklich?»

«Ja, wirklich. Wir verwenden das Second Conditional, wenn wir über eine Situation in der Gegenwart sprechen, die vollständig unwahr oder sehr unwahrscheinlich ist.»

«Okay, aber wenn ich du wäre, würde ich Leuten nicht sagen, dass sie wie Mr Bean aussehen. Sie könnten ziemlich ärgerlich werden und dir eins auf die Nase geben.»

«Bist du ich?»

"Am I you? No! I was just saying that *if I were you* ... Oh I get you, another case of the second conditional."

"You have to admit that it is pretty unlikely that you will ever be me."

"Thank goodness!"

"Don't be so cheeky. You're lucky that you wear glasses."

"Why's that?"

"Well, *if you didn't wear* glasses, *I'd punch* you on the nose!"

"I thought you didn't approve of violence."

"Okay, *if I approved* of violence and *if you didn't wear* glasses, *I would punch* you on the nose!"

"Did you see what I did?"

"What did you do?"

"I elicited two examples of the second conditional out of you."

"Well done, Barry. You are learning. Did you notice that in the second conditional the verb form after the 'If' is in the past tense?"

"If I looked ..."

"Exactly. But we are not talking about the past. We're talking about now. But simply a situation that is ..."

"... in the present but is plainly untrue, or very unlikely – the second conditional!"

"Exactly. A lot of foreign students have problems with that."

«Bin ich du? Nein! Ich habe lediglich gesagt, wenn ich du wäre … Oh, jetzt verstehe ich. Das ist ein anderes Beispiel für das Second Conditional.»

«Du musst zugeben, dass es ziemlich unwahrscheinlich ist, dass du jemals ich sein wirst.»

«Gott sei Dank.»

«Sei nicht so frech. Du kannst froh sein, dass du eine Brille trägst.»

«Warum?»

«Nun, wenn du keine Brille tragen würdest, würde ich dir eins auf die Nase geben!»

«Ich dachte, du hättest etwas gegen Gewalt.»

«Okay. Wenn ich nichts gegen Gewalt hätte und du keine Brille tragen würdest, dann würde ich dir eins auf die Nase geben!»

«Ist dir etwas aufgefallen?»

«Was meinst du?»

«Ich habe zwei Beispiele des Second Conditional aus dir herausgelockt.»

«Gut gemacht, Barry. Du lernst allmählich. Hast du gemerkt, dass im Second Conditional das Verb nach dem ‹if› im Imperfekt steht?»

«If I looked …»

«Richtig. Aber wir sprechen nicht über die Vergangenheit. Wir sprechen über das, was gerade ist. Einfach über eine Situation, die …»

«… in der Gegenwart ist, aber vollständig unwahr ist, oder unwahrscheinlich – das Second Conditional!»

«Genau. Viele ausländische Studenten haben Probleme damit.»

"The Great … People who pay my wages."

"Exactly. You can probably see the basic structure, if blah blah blah, I would blah blah blah."

"Yep, I can see that."

"Some foreigners, particularly German students, often put the 'if' and the 'would' in the same part of the sentence. If I would look like Mr Bean …"

"If I would? Even I can see that there's something wrong there."

"Good to hear. Of course you can often turn the sentence around. I would cry myself to sleep …"

"… if I looked like Mr Bean. Which I don't."

"Correct."

"One quick question. We've looked at the zero, first and second conditional forms. How many are there exactly?"

"Well, nobody knows exactly …"

"Nobody knows? You mean, no one has actually researched something as basic as conditional forms?"

"They're actually very complicated; far more complicated than the average textbook lets on."

"So, go on, how many are there? Six? Ten?"

"I heard of a researcher who found two hundred and fifty-six different conditional forms."

«Pö… Die Leute, die mein Gehalt zahlen.»

«Stimmt. Du kannst wahrscheinlich die grundlegende Struktur erkennen. Also … if … blablabla, I would blablabla …»

«Ja, verstehe.»

«Viele Ausländer, und ganz besonders deutsche Schüler, nehmen gerne das ‹if› und das ‹would› im gleichen Teil des Satzes, also ‹If I would look like Mr Bean …›»

«If I would? Sogar ich sehe, dass das so nicht stimmen kann.»

«Das höre ich gern. Natürlich kannst du den Satz auch herumdrehen: ‹Ich würde mich jeden Abend in den Schlaf heulen …»

«…sähe ich aus wie Mr Bean. Was ich aber nicht tue.»

«Richtig.»

«Noch eine kurze Frage. Wir haben uns bereits das Zero, das First und das Second Conditional angeschaut. Wie viele gibt es genau?»

«Nun, das weiß niemand so genau …»

«Das weiß niemand? Du meinst, niemand hat bisher so was Grundlegendes wie die Formen des Conditional näher untersucht?»

«Diese sind ziemlich kompliziert. Deutlich komplizierter, als Lehrbücher es vermuten lassen.»

«Und? Wie viele gibt es? Sechs? Zehn?»

«Ich habe von einem Forscher gehört, der zweihundertsechsundfünfzig unterschiedliche Formen des Conditional gefunden haben will.»

"Two hundred and fifty-six ! ! ! ! !"

"It's quite a lot, isn't it? Most textbooks will tell students that there are only three or four."

"Ah, that sounds better."

"Yes, but that is not the real world. Penny Ur, a TEFL guru, did a bit of research and found one hundred cases of conditional forms in her Sunday paper. Only twenty-seven percent conformed to the four most commonly taught forms."

"Well, teachers and textbook writers are clearly teaching the wrong ones !"

"I'm not sure about that but a lot more has to be done to make students aware that there is more to conditionality than the four basic forms."

"So are we going to do two hundred and fifty-six different ones today?"

"Er, no. Today, I'm going to teach you about the four basic forms. It is then up to you to go out and find out about the other two hundred and fifty-two !"

"Gee thanks. *If I had known* how difficult English grammar was *I wouldn't have come* on this bloody course."

"But you're on it now."

"Very observant of you, Grasshopper !"

"So you were talking about a hypothetical situation, like the second conditional, only this time, it is an event which occurred in the past and therefore cannot be changed."

«Zweihundertsechsundfünfzig?!»

«Das sind ziemlich viele, oder? Die meisten Lehrbücher beschreiben nur drei oder vier.»

«Das hört sich schon besser an.»

«Ja, aber das ist nicht die Realität. Penny Ur, ein TEFL-Guru, hat ein wenig nachgeforscht und hundert verschiedene Formen des Conditional in ihrer Sonntagszeitung gefunden. Nur siebenundzwanzig Prozent stimmten mit den vier am häufigsten gelehrten überein.»

«Nun, wie es aussieht, vermitteln Lehrer und Lehrbuchautoren wohl die falschen!»

«Da bin ich mir nicht sicher, aber es muss bestimmt mehr getan werden, damit Schüler mehr als die vier grundlegenden Formen des Conditional kennen.»

«Wir besprechen heute also alle zweihundertsechsundfünfzig?»

«Nein, machen wir nicht. Ich stelle dir die vier grundlegenden Formen vor. Du kannst dich dann selbst über die anderen zweihundertzweiundfünfzig schlaumachen.»

«Na super. Hätte ich gewusst, wie schwierig die englische Grammatik ist, dann hätte ich diesen verdammten Kurs niemals belegt.»

«Hast du aber.»

«Gut beobachtet, du Schlaumeier!»

«Du hast jetzt über eine hypothetische Situation gesprochen, so wie im Second Conditional. Nur ist es dieses Mal eine Handlung, die in der Vergangenheit liegt und daher nicht mehr geändert werden kann.»

"Fancy language but I think the facts were right."

"So you were expressing regret."

"Yep. My sister's in Torremolinos at the moment. *If I hadn't come* on this course, *I would have flown out* with her."

"But you didn't fly out with her."

"No, I just told you that, bird brain."

"I was just asking a checking question."

"Oh, I'm sorry. *If I had known* you were asking me a checking question, *I wouldn't have called* you bird brain."

"Brilliant!"

"What was?"

"Yet another example of the *third conditional*!"

"So what is my model sentence for the *third conditional*?"

"I think your first one: *If I had known how difficult English grammar was, I wouldn't have come on this bloody course.*"

«Originell ausgedrückt, aber die Fakten stimmen.»

«Du bedauerst es also?»

«Ja, meine Schwester ist gerade in Torremolinos. Hätte ich diesen Kurs nicht belegt, dann wäre ich mit ihr dorthin geflogen.»

«Aber du bist nicht mit ihr geflogen.»

«Nein, habe ich dir doch gerade gesagt, Spatzenhirn.»

«Ich wollte mich nur vergewissern.»

«Entschuldigung. Hätte ich gewusst, dass du dich nur vergewissern wolltest, dann hätte ich dich nicht ‹Spatzenhirn› genannt.»

«Genial!»

«Was?»

«Nochmals ein Beispiel für das Third Conditional!»

«Welchen Satz soll ich als Beispielsatz für das Third Conditional nehmen?»

«Ich denke, deinen ersten: ‹Hätte ich gewusst, wie schwierig die englische Grammatik ist, dann hätte ich diesen verdammten Kurs niemals belegt.›»

"Very true."

"Okay, I think it's time for another table. Can you make one?"

"I speak English but I don't know it. The more I study it the more I find out that I don't know. I just feel overwhelmed by all this continuous present perfect passive zero conditional … why can't we all speak Esperanto? Now if everybody spoke Esperanto …"

"You and I would be out of a job."

"Point taken. So you mentioned hair conditioner earlier."

"I did."

"*If someone uses* hair conditioner *their hair looks* lovely."

"And which conditional is that?"

« Wie wahr. »

« Gut. Ich denke, es ist Zeit für eine neue Tabelle. Stellst du eine zusammen? »

NAME	KONSTRUK-TION	VERWEN-DUNG	BEISPIEL-SATZ
Second Conditional	If+Past Tense + would + Present Tense	eine Situation in der Gegenwart, die entweder falsch oder höchst unwahrscheinlich ist	If I looked like Mr Bean, I would cry myself to sleep every night.
Third Conditional	If+had+Past Participle + Past Tense + would + have + Past Participle	wenn man über etwas spricht, das in der Vergangenheit hätte eintreten können, aber jetzt, also in der Gegenwart, nicht mehr eintreten kann	If I had known how difficult English grammar was, I wouldn't have come on this bloody course.

« Ich spreche Englisch, aber ich weiß eigentlich nichts darüber. Je mehr ich erfahre, desto deutlicher sehe ich, dass ich nichts kann. Ich bin total erschlagen von all diesem Continuous Present Perfect Passive Zero Conditional … Warum können nicht alle Esperanto sprechen? Wenn alle Esperanto sprächen … »

« Dann wären du und ich arbeitslos. »

« Verstanden! Du hast vorhin von Conditioner gesprochen. »

« Ja, habe ich. »

« Wenn man Conditioner verwendet, sieht das Haar schön aus. »

« Und welches Conditional ist das? »

"The zero conditional!"

"Great start."

"If you let me use your expensive hair conditioner I'll be eternally grateful."

"Which is the …"

"First conditional!"

"Bingo."

"If I stopped using hair conditioner my hair would lose its wonderful shine."

"Lovely example of the …"

"Second conditional!"

"You're on fire!"

"No, I'm not. But if I was on fire I would jump in the river. Ha ha."

"Ah, now you've opened up a can of worms."

"No, not a can of worms, I was talking about hair conditioner."

"You said: 'If I was on fire …'."

"I would jump in the river. Second conditional!"

"Is it 'If I was on fire …' or 'If I were on fire …'?"

"Well I would say 'If I was on fire …' Is that wrong?"

"As you know I'm not a fan of the word 'wrong'. Many native speakers say 'If I was …' Plenty of native speakers say 'If I were …'."

"So what am I supposed to say if a German student asks me, teacher, which one is correct?"

"You can tell them that they are both accept-

«Das Zero Conditional!»

«Das ist schon mal ein guter Anfang.»

«Wenn du mich deinen teuren Conditioner verwenden lässt, dann werde ich dir ewig dankbar sein.»

«Und das hier wäre dann …»

«Das First Conditional!»

«Bingo.»

«Würde ich keinen Conditioner mehr verwenden, würde mein Haar seinen schönen Glanz verlieren.»

«Das ist ein nettes Beispiel zum …»

«Second Conditional!»

«Nun hat es gezündet!»

«Nein, hat es nicht. Wenn es gezündet hätte, würde ich jetzt zum Löschen in den Fluss springen. Haha.»

«Nun hast du in ein Wespennest gestochen.»

«Nein, kein Wespennest. Ich habe nur über Conditioner gesprochen.»

«Du hast gesagt: ‹Wenn es gezündet hätte …›»

«… würde ich in den Fluss springen, Second Conditional!»

«Heißt es ‹If I was on fire …› oder ‹If I were on fire …›?»

«Ich würde sagen: ‹If I was on fire …› Ist das falsch?»

«Wie du weißt, bin ich nicht gerade ein Anhänger des Wortes ‹falsch›. Viele Muttersprachler sagen ‹If I was …› Und viele sagen auch ‹If I were …›»

«Was soll ich dann sagen, wenn mich ein deutscher Schüler fragt, welche der beiden Formen korrekt ist?»

«Du kannst sagen, dass beide Formen richtig sind,

able though there are some expressions where 'If I was' sounds strange and most people avoid it."

"Such as?"

"*If I were you …*"

"That's 'cause it's like a little expression."

"The technical word is 'chunk' but you're right."

"'If I was you' just doesn't sound right."

"A lot of people use it – though '*If I were you*' is about six times more common in written form."

"Thanks for your brilliant explanation – though you did interrupt my lovely hair conditioner examples."

"I apologise."

"Apology accepted. If you hadn't interrupted me I would have given you another sentence about hair conditioner!"

"Nice one. Now which conditional did you just use?"

"The third conditional!"

"Brilliant. *If I were you I'd make* a little summary so you don't forget the basic conditional structures."

"Well, I am me and I'm going to take your excellent advice."

dass es aber ein paar stehende Wendungen gibt, bei denen sich ‹If I was› seltsam anhört, und die meisten Leute dies nicht verwenden.»

«Und was zum Beispiel?»

«If I were you …»

«So sagt man das.»

«Der technische Ausdruck hierfür wäre ‹chunk›, aber du hast recht.»

«‹If I was you› hört sich einfach nicht richtig an.»

«Viele Leute verwenden es, aber ‹If I were you› ist im schriftlichen Englisch ungefähr sechsmal häufiger als im gesprochenen.»

«Vielen Dank für die Aufklärung – aber du hast mich bei meinen schönen Beispielen mit den Conditionern unterbrochen.»

«Entschuldige.»

«Entschuldigung angenommen. Hättest du mich nicht unterbrochen, hätte ich dir noch einen weiteren Satz über Conditioner geliefert!»

«Schönes Beispiel. Welche Form des Conditional ist das?»

«Das Third Conditional!»

«Super. Wenn ich du wäre, würde ich jetzt eine kleine Zusammenfassung machen, so dass du die grundlegenden Conditional-Strukturen nicht vergisst.»

«Nun, ich bin ich und werde deinen guten Rat annehmen.»

Summary

Zero conditional:

If I heat water to hundred degrees Celsius, it boils!

First conditional:

If you pour concrete over your flowers, they will die!

Second conditional:

If I looked like Mr Bean I would cry myself to sleep every night.

Third conditional:

If I had known how difficult English grammar was, I wouldn't have come on this bloody course.

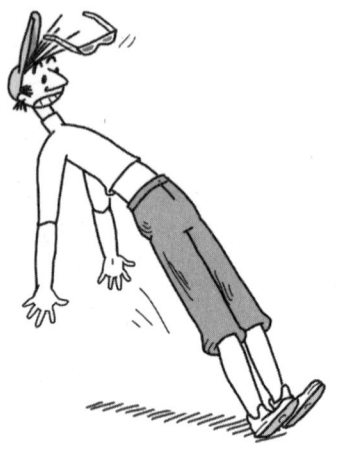

Zusammenfassung

Zero Conditional:
Wenn ich Wasser auf hundert Grad Celsius erhitze, kocht es!

First Conditional:
Wenn du Beton über deine Blumen gießt, werden sie sterben!

Second Conditional:
Sähe ich wie Mr Bean aus, würde ich mich jeden Abend in den Schlaf heulen.

Third Conditional:
Hätte ich gewusst, wie schwierig die englische Grammatik ist, dann hätte ich diesen verdammten Kurs niemals belegt.

Propositions with Prepositions

"Hi, Barry. Today I'd like to have a look at prepositions."

"You mean when you say to someone, 'Do you come here often?' or 'Have you got a head-ache from when you fell out of heaven?' or my favourite, 'Do you want to come up to see my butterfly collection?'"

"Those are propositions – and probably the worst propositions I've heard in years. No, today we'll be looking at prepositions."

"Okay, great teacher, please enlighten me as to the nature of these prepositions of which you speak."

"Wow, it sounds like you've just walked out of a Jane Austen novel."

"Well, I'm off to Germany soon and I want to talk proper English."

"So do you think 'proper' English is modern

Anmache mit Präpositionen

«Hallo, Barry. Heute wollen wir uns einmal die Präpositionen ansehen.»

«Meinst du solche wie ‹Kommst du häufig hierher?› oder ‹Hast du Kopfschmerzen bekommen, als du vom Himmel gefallen bist?› oder mein Lieblingsbeispiel ‹Willst du mit raufkommen, dann zeig ich dir meine Schmetterlingssammlung?›»

«Das ist Anmache und nebenbei auch mit vom Schlimmsten, was ich seit Langem gehört habe. Das war nicht gemeint. Wir schauen uns heute Präpositionen an.»

«Also gut, Herr Lehrer, lassen Sie mich bitte mehr über das Wesen dieser Präpositionen wissen.»

«Beeindruckend. Das hört sich an, als kämst du geradewegs aus einem Jane-Austen-Roman.»

«Nun, bald geht es nach Deutschland, und ich will richtiges Englisch sprechen.»

«Ist für dich ‹richtiges› Englisch modernes Englisch,

English spoken by native speakers or English as it was written by Jane Austen more than two hundred years ago?"

"The first one – which is great 'cause I don't know nothing about proper English."

"You don't know …"

"Anything. I know – I was just trying to make a joke. Anyway, back to these propositions."

"Prepositions!"

"Exactly. So, what are they?"

"Prepositions are words or phrases which show a relationship between two things in space or time."

"Could you say that in English please?"

"It's probably best if we give some examples. Where's your bag? I can't see it."

"It's there, *on* the table."

"Oh yes, I can see it now. But where is your pot noodle? I know you always bring a pot noodle to class."

"It's *in* my bag. Listen, you're supposed to be teaching me about prepositions and you're asking some pretty weird questions."

"There is method in my madness."

"I wonder about that sometimes."

"What time do you get up?"

"About eight o'clock."

"Which one?"

"Which one? Oh I see. Eight o'clock *in* the morning of course."

das von Muttersprachlern gesprochen wird, oder Englisch, wie es von Jane Austen vor mehr als zweihundert Jahren geschrieben wurde?»

«Ersteres – das ist gut, denn ich weiß nicht nichts von richtigem Englisch.»

«Was weißt du nicht?»

«Nichts. Hab schon verstanden. Ich wollte nur einen Witz machen. Zurück zur Anmache.»

«Zu den Präpositionen!»

«Genau. Also, was hat es damit auf sich?»

«Präpositionen sind Wörter oder Formulierungen, die eine Beziehung zwischen zwei Dingen in Raum und Zeit erkennen lassen.»

«Kannst du das nochmal so sagen, dass ich es verstehe?»

«Es ist wohl am besten, wenn wir ein paar Beispiele bringen. Wo ist deine Tasche? Ich kann sie nicht sehen.»

«Sie ist da, auf dem Tisch.»

«Stimmt, jetzt sehe ich sie. Aber wo ist deine 5-Minuten-Terrine? Ich weiß, dass du immer eine zum Unterricht mitbringst.»

«Sie ist in meiner Tasche. Hör mal, du sollst mir doch etwas über Präpositionen beibringen, und dabei stellst du mir ein paar ziemlich blöde Fragen.»

«Meine Methode hat System.»

«Ich frage mich immer wieder, ob das stimmt.»

«Um wie viel Uhr stehst du auf?»

«Gegen acht Uhr.»

«Acht Uhr was?»

«Acht Uhr was? Oh ja, verstehe. Um acht Uhr am Morgen natürlich.»

"Very good. And when do you have your afternoon nap?"

"Trick question!"

"Nothing tricky, just super simple."

"*In* the afternoon."

"Excellent."

"I see a pattern here – *in* the morning, *in* the afternoon …"

"Very good, so the answer to my next question is …?"

"*In* the evening!"

"Brilliant. I didn't need to ask you when you lie on the sofa, watch telly and eat pop tarts."

"So is '*in* the morning' a preposition?"

"No, it isn't. The word 'the' is a definite article. The word 'morning' is a noun. But the word '*in*'…"

"… is a preposition?"

"Correct! Where's your pot noodle?"

"I told you that already. Wait a minute, it's *in* my bag!"

"And where's your bag?"

"*On* the table! So '*on*' is a preposition as well?"

"It is."

"So there are two prepositions!"

"There are actually over hundred, but don't worry too much about them."

"A hundred! Is there a list of them somewhere that I can look at?"

"You could but it won't help you – or learners of English very much."

« Sehr gut. Und wann machst du deinen Mittags-schlaf? »

« Fangfrage! »

« Nichts dergleichen! »

« Am Nachmittag. »

« Prima. »

« Ich kann hier ein Muster erkennen – am Morgen, am Nachmittag … »

« Sehr gut. Und die Antwort auf meine nächste Frage lautet …? »

« Am Abend! »

« Ausgezeichnet. Ich musste dich also nicht fragen, wann du auf dem Sofa liegst, fernsiehst und Pop-Tarts isst. »

« Ist also ‹am Morgen› eine Präposition? »

« Nein. ‹Morgen› ist ein Substantiv, aber das Wort ‹am› (an in Verbindung mit einem bestimmten Artikel) ist … »

« … eine Präposition? »

« Richtig! Wo ist deine 5-Minuten-Terrine? »

« Das hab ich dir doch schon gesagt. Ah, verstehe, sie ist in meiner Tasche! »

« Und wo ist deine Tasche? »

« Auf dem Tisch! ‹Auf› ist also auch eine Präposition? »

« Stimmt! »

« Es gibt also zwei Präpositionen. »

« Es gibt eigentlich über hundert, aber da mach dir mal keinen Kopf. »

« Einhundert! Gibt es irgendwo eine Liste, die ich mir anschauen kann? »

« Gibt es, aber es wird dir – oder denjenigen, die Eng-lisch lernen, wenig helfen. »

"Why not?"

"Well, some prepositions are pretty easy, *on* the table, *in* your bag, *under* the book, *behind* the bike sheds …"

"Where I had my first kiss!"

"Why am I not surprised? There are lots which don't seem to follow a pattern. You get up at eight o'clock …"

"*In* the morning!"

"You have your afternoon nap …"

"*In* the afternoon!"

"You lie on the sofa, watch telly and eat pop tarts …"

"*In* the evening!"

"You sleep …"

"*In* the … wait a minute, *at* night. *At* night? Why did they change it?"

"There is no 'they' for the English language. Language evolves, picks up bits from other languages and it all comes together …"

"As a kind of mish-mash."

"Yes, but a very beautiful mish-mash. Now one big problem area for lots of foreign learners of English is which preposition to use after particular verbs."

"I think I need an example."

"You told me that you worked by Poundland."

"By Poundland? No, I worked *for* Poundland."

«Warum nicht?»

«Nun, einige Präpositionen sind relativ einfach, so
wie auf dem Tisch, in deiner Tasche, unter dem Buch,
hinter dem Fahrradschuppen …»

«Wo ich meinen ersten Kuss bekam!»

«Was mich nicht überrascht! Es gibt viele, die keinem
bestimmten Muster folgen. Du stehst um acht Uhr
auf …»

«Am Morgen!»

«Du machst deinen Mittagsschlaf …»

«Am Nachmittag!»

«Du liegst auf dem Sofa, siehst fern und isst Pop-
Tarts …»

«Am Abend!»

«Du schläfst …»

«Am … wart mal … in der Nacht. In der Nacht?
Warum haben sie das geändert?»

«Da gibt es kein ‹sie›. Sprache entwickelt sich, nimmt
Teile aus anderen Sprachen auf, und so kommt alles zusammen zu …»

«… einer Art Mischmasch.»

«Stimmt. Aber zu einem sehr schönen Mischmasch.
Viele Leute, die Englisch als Fremdsprache lernen, haben
besondere Probleme bei der Verwendung von Präpositionen nach bestimmten Verben.»

«Ich glaube, ein Beispiel wäre gut.»

«Du hast mir gesagt, dass du in Poundland gearbeitet
hast.»

«In Poundland? Nein, ich habe bei Poundland gearbeitet.»

"Ah, so we have to say 'work for'?"

"Yes."

"Thank you. I'm not very good in prepositions."

"Not very good *at* prepositions!"

"Ah, so we say 'good at', 'bad at' 'interested at'…"

"No, we say 'interested *in*'!"

"Why, Mr Buggins, why?"

"Because the English language is a very beautiful mish-mash."

"I don't think your German students will appreciate that answer."

"So what should I tell them?"

"Encourage them to learn language in chunks rather than individual words."

"Er, yeah, for example …"

«Es heißt also ‹arbeiten bei›?»

«Ja.»

«Danke. Ich bin nicht so besonders gut bei Präpositionen.»

«Nicht so, (allenfalls) ‹gut in Präpositionen›!»

«Ach so, wir sagen also ‹gut in›, ‹schlecht in›, ‹interessiert in› …»

«Nein, es heißt ‹interessiert an›!»

«Wieso, Mr Buggins?»

«Weil die englische Sprache ein sehr schöner Mischmasch ist.»

«Ich glaube nicht, dass sich deine deutschen Studenten mit dieser Antwort zufriedengeben.»

«Was soll ich ihnen dann sagen?»

«Ermutige sie, feststehende Wendungen zu lernen anstatt einzelner Wörter.»

«Äh, hast du ein Beispiel für mich?»

"Afraid of, interested in, in front of, at a party …"

"Wow, there are loads!"

"There are. The good news is that if a German tells you she met her husband on a party you can still understand what she's trying to say."

"She met her husband *at* a party."

"Exactly. Interestingly, if you stay in Germany for a long while you will hear the wrong version so many times that it starts to sound totally normal. 'I spent the weekend by my parents.' What's wrong with that?"

"We don't say that … do we?"

"No we don't – I spent the weekend *with* my parents, but once you've heard it a thousand times then it is hard for your brain not to accept it as correct."

"Oh, I don't think I'll have a problem with that. My brain is pretty special."

"Oh yes, of that I have no doubt."

"So can you tell me more about these 'chunks' with prepositions. Sounds like they're pretty important."

"Sure. Where is your niece for most of her time from Monday to Friday?"

"*At* school – the poor thing."

"Is she the worst pupil in her class?"

"No way! I reckon she's probably at the top of the class!"

«Angst vor, interessiert an, vor etwas, auf einer Party …»

«Beeindruckend. Das sind ja einige.»

«Stimmt. Das Gute daran ist, dass du, wenn eine Deutsche dir erzählt, dass sie ihren Mann in einer Party kennengelernt hat, trotzdem verstehen wirst, was sie meint.»

«Sie hat ihren Mann auf einer Party kennengelernt.»

«Genau. Nun ist es aber so, dass du, wenn du eine Zeit lang in Deutschland gewohnt hast, so oft die falsche Version gehört hast, dass sich solche Dinge dann ganz normal anhören. ‹I spent the weekend by my parents.› Was ist hier falsch?»

«So sagen wir das nicht, oder?»

«Nein, machen wir nicht. Wir sagen ‹I spent the weckend with my parents›. Aber wenn du das andere tausendmal gehört hast, wird es deinem Kopf schwerfallen, es nicht als richtig zu empfinden.»

«Ach, ich glaube nicht, dass ich ein Problem damit haben werde. Mein Kopf ist ziemlich speziell.»

«Daran habe ich keinen Zweifel.»

«Kannst du mir noch etwas mehr über diese feststehenden Wendungen sagen? Hört sich für mich so an, als ob die ziemlich wichtig wären.»

«Sicher. Wo verbringt deine Nichte zwischen Montag und Freitag die meiste Zeit?»

«In der Schule, das arme Ding.»

«Ist sie die schlechteste Schülerin ihrer Klasse?»

«Absolut nicht! Ich glaube sogar, dass sie ist eine der Besten ist!»

"When did she start school?"

"*At* the age of five."

"What time does school start?"

"*At* nine o'clock."

"Does she go to school on the weekend?"

"You mean at the weekend!"

"Oh, did I do a mistake?"

"Not do a mistake, *make* a mistake!"

"Thanks for that. Now, Barry, I hear your brother is an investment guru."

"Well, he buys stocks and shares online."

"Wow, I wish I could do that. It must be really difficult."

"Nah, it's actually pretty easy."

"It is?"

"Yeah, all you have to do is to buy at a low price and sell at a high price."

"Buy at a low price, sell at a high price? Wow, I think I might become an investment guru as well. I imagine your brother is really good on it."

"Good *at* it!"

"Oops, I made another mistake. At least I can laugh on my mistakes."

"Laugh *at* your mistakes!"

"Oh well, on the end of the day …"

"*At* the end of the day!"

"Another mistake. I hope you're not angry at me."

"I'm angry *with* you!"

"So I can't say 'angry at'?"

«Wann hat sie mit der Schule angefangen?»

«Im Alter von fünf.»

«Um wie viel Uhr fängt die Schule an?»

«Um neun Uhr.»

«Geht sie im Wochenende zur Schule?»

«Du meinst wohl am Wochenende!»

«Ups, habe ich einen Fehler getan?»

«Nicht einen Fehler tun, sondern machen!»

«Danke dir. Nun, Barry, ich habe gehört, dein Bruder sei ein Investmentguru.»

«Nun, er kauft Aktien und Anteile online.»

«Super. Ich wünschte, ich könnte das auch. Das muss richtig schwierig sein.»

«Nee, es ist eigentlich ziemlich leicht.»

«Wirklich?»

«Ja. Du musst nur eine Aktie zu einem niedrigen Kurs kaufen und zu einem höheren Kurs verkaufen.»

«Zu einem niedrigen Kurs kaufen und zu einem höheren verkaufen? Wow, ich denke, ich werde auch ein Investmentguru. Ich kann mir denken, dass dein Bruder wirklich gut dabei ist.»

«Gut darin!»

«Ups, da habe ich wieder einen Fehler gemacht. Zumindest kann ich auf meine Fehler lachen.»

«Über deine Fehler lachen!»

«Na gut, beim Ende des Tages ...»

«Am Ende des Tages!»

«Noch ein Fehler. Ich hoffe, du bist nicht böse mit mir.»

«Ich bin böse auf dich!»

«Ich kann also nicht ‹böse mit› sagen?»

"Well, you can …"

"But I can also say 'angry with'?"

"Definitely."

"So, Barry Buggins, native speaker, trained English teacher, explain when to use 'angry with' and when to use 'angry at'."

"That is an excellent question and I'll get back to you on that one."

"You can only use that excuse a few times before your students lose faith in you completely. Sorry is it 'lose faith in' or 'lose faith at'?"

"*Lose faith in*!"

"And why?"

"'cause it just is!"

"'cause it just is'. Ah thank you, great teacher. I am so happy that I have paid a lot of money to come to take lessons from you and I get pearls of wisdom like 'cause it just is' when I ask a question."

"Maybe this English teaching thing is not for me. I need to know everything and it seems I know almost nothing."

"Don't be too *hard on* yourself, Barry. Nobody knows everything. The more you work at it, the better at it you'll be."

"Work at, better at, laugh at, angry at, at the end of the day, sell at, buy at, good at, at nine o'clock. at the age of five, at the top … these are all chunks – using the preposition 'at'!"

«Nun ja, du kannst … »

«Aber ich kann auch ‹böse auf› sagen? »

«Auf jeden Fall. »

«Nun, Barry Buggins, Muttersprachler, ausgebildeter Englischlehrer, erkläre mir bitte, wann du ‹böse mit› und wann du ‹böse auf› verwendest. »

«Das ist eine ausgezeichnete Frage, und ich werde darauf zurückkommen. »

«Diese Entschuldigung kannst du nur ein paarmal bringen, bevor deine Studenten den Glauben an dich verlieren. Was, denkst du, sagt man im Englischen, den Glauben an dich verlieren oder den Glauben in dich verlieren? »

«Den Glauben an etwas verlieren ! »

«Und warum? »

«Weil es einfach so ist ! »

«‹Weil es einfach so ist.› Danke dir, mein großartiger Lehrer. Ich bin so glücklich, dass ich so viel Geld für Unterricht bei dir bezahlt habe und alles, was ich als Antwort auf meine Fragen bekomme, sind Perlen der Weisheit wie ‹weil es einfach so ist›. »

«Vielleicht ist das mit dem Englischlehrer doch nichts für mich. Ich muss alles wissen, und es scheint, ich kann fast gar nichts. »

«Geh nicht so hart mit dir ins Gericht, Barry. Niemand kann alles wissen. Je mehr du lernst, desto mehr weißt du. »

«Work at, better at, laugh at, angry at, at the end of the day, sell at, buy at, good at, at nine o'clock, at the age of five, at the top … das sind alles Wörter, die in Verbindung mit der Präposition ‹at› verwendet werden. »

"They are indeed, Barry. We're making progress."

"I'm *good at* using 'at' !"

"Native speakers usually are. Okay, let's move on. Where are you going after class today?"

"*To the cinema* !"

"Really? What are you going to see?"

"'*Back to* the future !'"

"How convenient. And how do I get to the cinema?"

"It's easy. You know where Greggs is? It's to the right of Greggs. Haven't you been to the cinema before?"

"Personally I prefer the theatre. Compared to cinema, theatre is in a class of its own."

"That reminds me, where does the word 'snob' come from?"

"It may have come from the Latin, sine nobilitate, meaning 'without nobility', similar to the French, 'sans noblesse'. Why do you ask?"

"Oh, nothing. I was just thinking."

"So, how long will you be *in the cinema*?"

"*From* about half seven *to* about half nine."

"To half nine or 'until' half nine?"

"Er, you could say either. Do you want to come? It's a brilliant film. I could speak to my mates …"

"I'm sure it is but I've been invited to play bridge with some friends."

"Sine nobilitate, meaning 'without nobility'. Have I got that right?"

« Stimmt genau, Barry. Wir machen Fortschritte. »

« Der Gebrauch von ‹ at › klappt schon ganz gut. »

« Bei Muttersprachlern ist das in der Regel so. Lass uns weitermachen. Wohin gehst du heute nach der Unterrichtsstunde? »

« Ins Kino! »

« Wirklich? Was schaust du an? »

« ‹ Zurück in die Zukunft ›! »

« Wie praktisch. Und wie komme ich zum Kino? »

« Das ist einfach. Weißt du, wo das Greggs ist? Rechts neben dem Greggs ist das Kino. Warst du noch nie dort? »

« Persönlich ziehe ich Theater vor. Im Vergleich zu Kino ist Theater eine Klasse für sich. »

« Da fällt mir ein: Woher kommt das Wort ‹ Snob ›? »

« Aus dem Lateinischen, sine nobilitate, was so viel bedeutet wie ‹ ohne Adel ›, ähnlich wie der französische Ausdruck ‹ sans noblesse ›. Warum fragst du? »

« Och nichts, ich habe nur … gedacht. »

« Wie lange wirst du im Kino sein? »

« Von halb acht bis ungefähr halb zehn. »

« Sagt man da ‹ to half nine › oder ‹ until half nine ›? »

« Hm. Du kannst beides sagen. Willst du mitkommen? Es ist ein hervorragender Film. Ich könnte mit meinen Freunden reden … »

« Sicherlich ist es ein hervorragender Film. Aber ich habe eine Einladung zum Bridge mit ein paar Freunden. »

« Sine nobilitate bedeutet ‹ ohne Adel ›. Habe ich das richtig verstanden? »

"You have."

"I've just got it!"

"You have?"

"To!"

"To?"

"Yes, all those dumb questions you were asking. You were getting me to use the word 'to' which, unless I am a complete idiot, is a preposition!"

"The two things are not mutually exclusive but I have to say: great work, Sherlock! You're right again. Do you remember some of the chunks we used with 'to'?"

"To the cinema, back to the future, to the right of Greggs, to half nine, compared to, speak to, invited to …"

"You have a great memory, Barry."

"Thank you. I read a book about memory by … um, I've forgotten."

"How convenient. Now what time do you think we should finish today?"

"Well, I need to be at the cinema *by about quarter past seven* so if we can finish by about five past?"

"That should be fine. And what time do you think you'll be in bed tonight?"

"Hard to say. The film should finish by half nine, then I might *go for* a drink in the King's Arms."

"The King's Arms? Where's that?"

«Ja, hast du.»

«Nun habe ich es!»

«Was hast du?»

«To!»

«To?»

«Ja, alle diese blöden Fragen, die du mir gestellt hast, waren zu nichts anderem gut, als mich dazu zu bringen, das Wort ‹to› zu verwenden, und das ist, wenn ich nicht ein kompletter Idiot bin, eine Präposition!»

«Diese zwei Dinge schließen sich nicht gegenseitig aus, aber ich muss sagen: Gut gemacht, Sherlock! Du hast wieder recht. Erinnerst du dich noch an ein paar Ausdrücke mit ‹to›?»

«To the cinema, back to the future, to the right of Greggs, to half nine, compared to, speak to, invited to …»

«Du hast ein gutes Gedächtnis Barry.»

«Danke dir. Ich habe ein Buch über Gedächtnis gelesen, von … ups, ich hab's vergessen.»

«Wie passend. Wann, denkst du, sollten wir heute den Unterricht beenden?»

«Nun, ich sollte gegen Viertel nach sieben am Kino sein. Wenn wir also ungefähr um fünf nach Schluss machen könnten?»

«Das sollte gehen. Und wann, denkst du, dass du heute ins Bett gehen wirst?»

«Schwer zu sagen. Der Film endet gegen halb zehn, danach gehe ich wahrscheinlich noch auf einen Drink ins King's Arms.»

«Das King's Arms? Wo ist das?»

"*By the river.*"

"Lovely."

"So, depending how long I stay there I could be in bed by eleven or by midnight."

"Are you going to drink alcohol *at the pub*?"

"Is the pope catholic?"

"I'll take that as a yes. So how are you going to get home? You're not going to drive, are you?"

"No way. I have a number of options."

"That's good."

"I could go *by tram*, that's the quickest. I could go *by bus*, that would be cheaper but takes longer. If it's after midnight the only way to get home is *by taxi* – but that is wickedly expensive."

"You could always go by foot."

"By foot? You mean *on foot*! Ah, I get you now. You tricked me into using lots of phrases with our next preposition: by!"

"You're definitely getting good at this. Isn't it strange that we say by bike, by plane, by train, by taxi, by bus, by tram but …"

"*On foot*! We don't say 'by foot' that would be stup… that wouldn't follow the accepted use of prepositions."

"You're learning. Can I say 'by walking'?"

"'By walking'? No way. That's completely wrong."

"That's a shame. I thought that *by walking* home instead of driving I could save money and stay fit at the same time."

«Am Fluss.»

«Hübsche Lage.»

«Je nachdem, wie lange ich dort bin, werde ich entweder gegen elf oder gegen Mitternacht im Bett sein.»

«Wirst du im Pub Alkohol trinken?»

«Ist der Papst katholisch?»

«Also ja. Wie wirst du dann nachhause kommen? Du wirst doch nicht Auto fahren, oder?»

«Auf keinen Fall. Ich habe verschiedene Möglichkeiten.»

«Gut so.»

«Ich könnte mit der Straßenbahn fahren, das geht am schnellsten. Oder mit dem Bus, das wäre billiger, würde aber länger dauern. Nach Mitternacht bleibt mir nur ein Taxi, aber das ist schrecklich teuer.»

«Du könntest auch gehen.»

«Bei Fuß? Du meinst zu Fuß gehen! Aha, nun verstehe ich. Du hast mich dazu gebracht, immer wieder die Präposition ‹by› zu verwenden.»

«Du machst dich wirklich. Ist es nicht seltsam, dass wir im Englischen by bike, by plane, by train, by taxi, by bus und by tram sagen, aber …»

«On foot, zu Fuß! Wir sagen nicht ‹by foot›. Das wäre du … das würde nicht den geltenden Präpositionsregeln folgen.»

«Du bist lernfähig. Können wir ‹by walking› sagen?»

«‹By walking?› Auf keinen Fall. Das ist vollkommen falsch.»

«Schade. Ich dachte, ich könnte sagen: ‹Wenn ich nachhause ginge, anstatt zu fahren, könnte ich Geld sparen und gleichzeitig fit bleiben.›»

"Well …"

"But I can't say that because it is 'completely wrong'. What a shame."

"Well, you can say it."

"I can? Even though it is 'completely wrong'?"

"Well, maybe it isn't hundred per cent completely wrong. There are some cases, such as in your example, when you can say 'by walking'."

"I'm happy to hear that. Right, now I've got some more questions for you."

"Great, I can't wait."

"I can see some anti-histamine tablets next to your pot noodle. Why are they there?"

"'Cause I suffer from hay fever of course."

"Okay, I didn't know that. But hay fever is just a little problem. It's just like a mini cold."

"It is far from being a little problem. Without these tablets my nose would be running faster than Usain Bolt."

"So it's not the same as a cold then?"

"No, it's completely different from a cold … wait a minute …"

"Yes?"

"From, from, from!"

"It sounds like you're trying to start a small moped."

"From! The next preposition you've got me using. Suffer from, far from, different from …"

"And we were just getting started. We didn't

«Na gut …»

«Aber das kann ich nicht, weil es ‹vollkommen falsch› ist. Schade.»

«Doch, du kannst das schon.»

«Kann ich? Obwohl es ‹vollkommen falsch› ist?»

«Nun, vielleicht ist es ja nicht ganz und gar falsch. Es gibt ein paar Fälle, so wie in deinem Beispiel, bei denen man ‹by walking› sagen kann.»

«Freut mich zu hören. Nun noch ein paar weitere Fragen.»

«Super. Ich kann es kaum erwarten.»

«Da liegen Antihistamintabletten neben deiner 5-Minuten-Terrine. Warum liegen sie da?»

«Weil ich Heuschnupfen habe.»

«Oh, das habe ich nicht gewusst. Aber Heuschnupfen ist nur ein kleines Problem. Es ist so etwas wie eine kleine Erkältung.»

«Es ist alles andere als ein kleines Problem. Ohne diese Tabletten würde meine Nase schneller laufen als Usain Bolt.»

«Es ist also nicht dasselbe wie eine Erkältung?»

«Nein, es ist etwas vollkommen anderes als … warte mal …»

«Ja?»

«From, from, from!»

«Das hört sich so an, als ob du gerade versuchen würdest, ein Mofa zu starten.»

«From! Da sind wir also bei der nächsten Präposition. Suffer from, far from, different from …»

«Und wir haben eben erst angefangen. Wir sind noch

get on to 'steal from', 'hide from' or even 'come from'.

"Well that one's easy. No one would get that one wrong, would they?"

"Well, … have you heard of someone called The Red Baron?"

"The Red Baron got 'I come from' wrong?"

"A little patience please, Barry. Who was this 'Red Baron'?"

"He was a First World War flying ace. He shot down eighty planes!"

"Interesting. 'Red Baron' is an unusual name, isn't it?"

"Nah, that wasn't his real name. His real name was Baron von Richthofen!"

"Ah, so 'von' means 'from' does it?"

"I guess so."

nicht bei ‹steal from›, ‹hide from› geschweige denn
‹come from›. »

« Das ist einfach. Niemand wird das hier falsch machen,
oder? »

« Na ja … hast du schon mal etwas vom Roten Baron
gehört? »

« Der Rote Baron hat ‹I come from› falsch gemacht? »

« Ein bisschen Geduld, Barry. Wer war denn der Rote
Baron? »

« Das war ein deutscher Jagdflieger im Ersten Welt-
krieg. Er hat achtzig Flugzeuge abgeschossen ! »

« Interessant. ‹Roter Baron› ist ein ungewöhnlicher
Name, nicht wahr? »

« Das war nicht sein richtiger Name. Sein richtiger war
Baron von Richthofen ! »

« Ah so, und ‹von› bedeutet im Englischen ‹from›, oder? »

« Stimmt. »

"Now you've learnt a bit of German. How do you say 'I come from England'?"

"Ich … komme … von … England!"

"I think you'll find it is 'ich komme aus England'."

"What? Why did they change it?"

"Who are 'they' and what is 'it'?"

"'They', the Germans, 'it' the translation of 'from'?"

"Ah, you'd like a convenient translation of every English word for a German word."

"Well, yeah. It can't be that hard, can it?"

"Oh, Barry. You have so much to learn."

"I guess you're probably right – again. Shall I make a table with all of the prepositional phrases?"

"Excellent idea."

PRÄPOSITION	VERWENDUNG
in	in the morning
	in the afternoon
	in the evening
	in my bag
	interested in
	lose faith in
	in the cinema
at	at night
	good at
	bad at
	at a party
	at school
	at the top
	at the age of five
	at nine o'clock
	laugh at your mistakes
	at the end of the day

«Nun hast du etwas Deutsch gelernt. Wie würdest du auf Deutsch ‹ I come from England › sagen? »

«Ich … komme … von … England! »

«Nein, nicht ganz. Es heißt ‹ich komme aus England›. »

«Was? Warum haben sie das geändert? »

«Wer ist ‹sie›, und was ist ‹das›? »

«‹Sie›, das sind die Deutschen, und ‹das› ist die Übersetzung von ‹from›? »

«Verstehe. Hättest wohl gern eine Eins-zu-eins-Übersetzung? »

«Ja bitte. Das kann doch nicht so schwierig sein, oder? »

«Oh, Barry. Du musst noch so viel lernen. »

«Wahrscheinlich hast du wieder recht. Soll ich eine Tabelle zu den Präpositionen machen? »

«Hervorragende Idee. »

PRÄPOSITION	VERWENDUNG
to	to the cinema to the right of Greggs Have you been to …? compared to from half seven to half nine speak to my mates to be invited to
on	on the table on foot
under	under the table
behind	behind the bike sheds

PRÄPOSITION	VERWENDUNG
by	by about quarter past seven
	by the river
	by tram
	by bus
	by taxi
	by bike
	by plane
	by September
	a book written by

"Like it?"

"I love it, Barry. I couldn't have done a better job myself."

"You see? I'm not just a pretty face!"

PRÄPOSITION	VERWENDUNG
from	suffer from hay fever far from being a little problem different from steal from hide from I come from
with	angry with to spend time with s. o.

« Gefällt dir das? »

« Ich bin begeistert, Barry. Ich hätte es nicht besser machen können. »

« Da siehst du's. Ich habe mehr zu bieten als ein hübsches Gesicht. »

Countable versus Uncountable Nouns

"Okay, Barry, before we start class, would you like a cup of tea or coffee?"

"I smell a rat. You're not normally this generous."

"Don't be so critical. Tea of coffee?"

"Tea please."

"Would you like some milk?"

"Just a drop."

"Sugar?"

"Three please."

"There you go."

"Thanks, I can still smell that rat though."

"Okay, I admit, there was a little rat."

"Go on."

"How many cups of tea have you had this week?"

"Present perfect!"

Zählbare und nicht zählbare Substantive

« Hallo, Barry. Hast du Lust auf eine Tasse Tee oder Kaffee, bevor wir mit dem Unterricht anfangen? »

« Das muss einen Haken haben. Du bist normalerweise nicht so großzügig. »

« Stell dich nicht so an. Tee oder Kaffee? »

« Tee, bitte. »

« Möchtest du etwas Milch? »

« Nur einen Tropfen. »

« Zucker? »

« Drei bitte. »

« Bitte schön. »

« Danke. Aber das Ganze hat doch einen Haken, oder? »

« Okay, ich geb's zu. Einen kleinen. »

« Mach weiter. »

« Wie viele Tassen Tee hast du diese Woche getrunken? »

« Present Perfect! »

"Well done. If you could just answer the question …"

"I drink a lot of tea, me. Five cups a day, so that means, I have drunk fifteen cups of tea this week. What about you? How much have you drunk?"

"I don't drink that much tea. I find the caffeine affects my blood pressure adversely."

"Er, excuse me, oh great master, I thought we're here to push back the frontiers of English Language Teaching, not discuss the adverse effect of caffeine on your blood pressure."

"There is method in my madness, oh simple one."

"Okay, I prostrate myself in awe of your superior knowledge."

"So back to your tea drinking habits. How much cups of tea do you drink every day?"

"Trick question ! ! !"

"Well spotted. So what is the correct form?"

"How *many* cups of tea do you drink every day?"

"Good, and why?"

"I don't know. It just sounds better."

"I'm afraid 'just sounding better' is not a satisfactory explanation for our foreign friends."

"Okay, so what's the rule?"

"I thought you enjoyed the deductive method."

"I do ! I do ! Okay, give me some more examples."

«Gut gemacht. Aber könntest du auf die Frage antworten?»

«Ich trinke viel Tee. Fünf Tassen am Tag. Daher habe ich diese Woche schon fünfzehn Tassen Tee getrunken. Und du? Wie viele hast du getrunken?»

«Ich trinke nicht so viel Tee. Ich habe das Gefühl, dass das meinen Blutdruck steigen lässt.»

«Oh, Entschuldigung großer Meister, ich dachte, wir sind hier, um mein Englisch aufzubessern und mich für den Englischunterricht fit zu machen, nicht, um den negativen Effekt von Koffein auf deinen Blutdruck zu diskutieren.»

«Meine Methode hat System, weißt du das nicht mehr, oh großer Geist!»

«Okay. Ich verbeuge mich in Ehrfurcht vor deinem überlegenen Wissen.»

«Zurück zu deinen Trinkgewohnheiten. Wie viel Tassen Tee trinkst du so am Tag?»

«Fangfrage!»

«Richtig. Wie heißt es also richtig?»

«Wie viele Tassen Tee trinkst du so am Tag?»

«Richtig. Und warum?»

«Ich weiß nicht. Es hört sich besser an.»

«Ich fürchte, ‹es hört sich besser an› ist keine zufriedenstellende Erklärung für unsere ausländischen Freunde.»

«Also gut. Wie heißt die Regel?»

«Ich dachte, du hättest Spaß daran, eine solche herzuleiten.»

«Hab ich ja! Hab ich ja! Gib mir noch ein paar Beispiele.»

"How many milks did you have in your tea."

"How many milks? What kind of … ha! Another trick question!"

"Right again, oh simple one. Why can't I say 'How many milks'?"

"Because you can't use numbers with milk. Milk is … milk."

"Very profound. Milk is milk, I must remember that one. So what you're saying is, I can't count milk: one milk, two milks, three milks etc."

"In my humble opinion. Perhaps it is used in American English or in Australia, or Ireland or South Africa, but I, in my terribly limited exposure to the English language, have not come across anyone counting milks …"

"Nor have I. So we agree that we cannot count milk which is why we ask 'how much milk would you like in your tea?'"

"We do."

"Can you think of anything else that we can't count?"

"So milk isn't the only case?"

"No, there are hundreds."

"How many exactly?"

"I don't know. I've never counted. I have a life."

"That's not what I've heard. Sorry! I shouldn't say nasty things about you. I'd like to borrow some money from you. I lost my bus fare."

«Wie viele Milch hattest du in deinem Tee?»

«Wie viele Milch? Was ist das … ! Eine weitere Fangfrage!»

«Schon wieder richtig, oh großer Geist. Warum kann ich nicht sagen ‹Wie viele Milch›?»

«Weil du Milch nicht zählen kannst. Milch ist … Milch.»

«Sehr tiefgründig. Milch ist Milch. Das muss ich mir merken. Was du also meinst, ist, dass ich Milch nicht zählen kann, eine Milch, zwei Milch, drei Milch usw.»

«Meiner bescheidenen Meinung nach. Vielleicht wird ‹milks› ja im amerikanischen Englisch, in Australien, Irland oder Südafrika verwendet. Ich habe aber noch keinen getroffen, der ‹milks› zählt; aber ich bin auch noch nicht so weit rumgekommen.»

«Ich auch nicht. Wir sind uns also einig, dass wir Milch nicht zählen können und deshalb fragen: ‹Wie viel Milch möchtest du in deinen Tee?›»

«Ja.»

«Fallen dir noch andere Dinge ein, die man nicht zählen kann?»

«Milch ist also kein Einzelfall?»

«Nein, es gibt Hunderte.»

«Wie viele genau?»

«Ich weiß nicht. Ich habe die Wörter noch nicht gezählt. Ich habe auch noch ein Privatleben.»

«Da habe ich aber was anderes gehört. Entschuldigung! Ich sollte lieber nett zu dir sein, ich wollte mir nämlich etwas Geld borgen. Ich habe mein Fahrgeld verloren.»

"Say that again!"

"I'm sorry! Oh great superior being. I am truly …"

"Not that bit. What would you like to borrow?"

"Some money, just £ 1.80 until …"

"Excellent."

"Well, I'm glad you're so enthusiastic."

"*Some* money."

"Yes, *some* money."

"Not two moneys, or five moneys."

"No, just £ 1.80. Wait a minute, I get you. I can't count money!"

"Exactly!"

"But hold on, hold on, my sister's a cashier. She spends all day counting money. You're wrong!"

"Ouch, Barry, that hurt."

"I didn't touch you. Oh, I get you, you meant metaphysically. Of course, you're never wrong."

"I am occasionally wrong and am ready to admit it. But back to the lesson, you thought that money is countable."

"But it … explain this delicate problem to me, oh great one."

"Let's do a mini role play."

"Great, I love role plays, me. Who am I?"

"Your sister."

"And?"

"I'd like you to count money."

«Sag das nochmal!»

«Entschuldigung bitte! Du Meister aller Meister. Ich bin …»

«Nicht das. Was willst du dir borgen?»

«Etwas Geld, nur £ 1.80 bis …»

«Ausgezeichnet.»

«Freut mich, dass dich das so begeistern kann.»

«Etwas Geld.»

«Ja, etwas Geld.»

«Nicht zwei Gelder oder fünf Gelder.»

«Nein, nur £ 1.80. Sekunde mal – ich hab's! Geld kann man nicht zählen!»

«Genau!»

«Aber, wart mal kurz. Meine Schwester ist Kassiererin. Sie ist den ganzen Tag am Geldzählen. Du irrst dich!»

«Autsch, Barry. Das tat weh.»

«Ich hab dich doch nicht berührt. Oh, verstehe, du meintest metaphysisch. Du hast wie immer recht.»

«Gelegentlich irre ich mich auch, und ich gebe das gerne zu. Aber zurück zum Thema. Du dachtest, Geld ist zählbar.»

«Aber es … erklär mir doch diese knifflige Sache, mein großer Meister.»

«Lass uns ein kleines Rollenspiel machen.»

«Prima. Das ist was für mich. Wer bin ich?»

«Deine Schwester.»

«Und?»

«Ich will, dass du Geld zählst.»

"Er, that's it?"

"Yes, that's it. This is not Broadway."

"Okay. Here I am, sitting at my desk, there's a big pile of money in front of me!"

"Only one pile?"

"No, no, there are three piles."

"Good, good, so start counting."

"Ten pounds, twenty pounds, thirty pounds …"

"Um, excuse me, what are you counting?"

"This, I mean, *these* piles of beautiful money in front of me. You told me to count it all!"

"But you said, 'Ten pounds, twenty pounds, thirty pounds …'."

"Right. Like you told me."

"But I asked you to count *money*."

"But pounds *are* money. They're the same thing, you … why are you looking at me like that?"

"There is a fundamental difference between the word 'pounds' and the word 'money'. We can say one pound, two pounds, three pounds, but we can't say, one money, two moneys, three moneys."

"Well, that's obvious. I didn't think I had to explain that."

"What may be obvious to you, may not be obvious to learners of English."

"I get you."

"What about advice?"

"What about it?"

"Is it countable or uncountable?"

«Und das soll alles sein?»

«Ja, das ist alles. Wir sind hier nicht am Broadway.»

«Gut. Ich bin hier, sitze an meinem Pult und habe einen großen Stapel Geld vor mir liegen!»

«Nur einen?»

«Nein, drei Stapel.»

«Gut, fang an zu zählen.»

«Zehn Pfund, zwanzig Pfund, dreißig Pfund …»

«Äh, entschuldige bitte, was zählst du da?»

«Das hier, ich meine diese Stapel mit wunderschönem Geld vor mir. Du hast gesagt, ich soll alles zählen!»

«Aber du hast ‹Zehn Pfund, zwanzig Pfund, dreißig Pfund› gesagt …»

«Stimmt. So, wie du gesagt hast.»

«Aber ich wollte, dass du Geld zählst.»

«Aber Pfund ist Geld. Das ist dasselbe. Warum schaust du mich so an?»

«Es gibt einen grundlegenden Unterschied zwischen dem Wort ‹Pfund› und dem Wort ‹Geld›. Wir können ‹ein Pfund›, ‹zwei Pfund›, ‹drei Pfund› sagen, aber wir können nicht ‹ein Geld›, ‹zwei Gelder› ‹drei Gelder› sagen.»

«Das ist doch offensichtlich. Ich dachte nicht, dass ich das erklären sollte.»

«Was für dich offensichtlich ist, gilt nicht unbedingt für diejenigen, die Englisch lernen.»

«Verstanden.»

«Wie ist es mit Rat?»

«Was ist damit?»

«Ist Rat zählbar oder nicht zählbar?»

"Er, countable!"

"Sure?"

"Sure, I'm sure. One piece of advice, two pieces of advice."

"But you're counting *pieces* of advice, not advices."

"Surely people learning English know that."

"No, they don't. You commonly hear, 'Please teacher, can you give me an advice?'."

"*Some* advice!"

"Exactly, but can you explain why?"

"Because I can't count advice, only *pieces* of advice!"

"I think we're finally getting somewhere. Furniture?"

"Er, uncountable! Some furniture, a piece of furniture!"

"Information?"

"Uncountable! Some information, a piece of information!"

"But be careful. In German information is countable. And what about cake?"

"Countable! One cake, two cakes, three cakes!"

"Sure?"

"Positive! This countable/uncountable is a piece of ... wait a minute."

"Yes?"

"I can count cakes, can't I?"

"You certainly can."

"But I can also say, 'some cake' or 'a piece of cake'."

«Hm, zählbar!»

«Bist du sicher?»

«Sicher bin ich sicher. Ein Ratschlag, zwei Ratschläge.»

«Ja, aber hier zählst du Ratschläge, nicht Rat.»

«Diejenigen, die Englisch lernen, wissen das doch.»

«Die wissen es nicht. Du hörst immer wieder: ‹Können Sie mir bitte einen Rat (an advice) geben?›»

«Im Englischen würde das ‹some advice› heißen!»

«Stimmt. Kannst du erklären, warum?»

«Weil man ‹Rat› nicht zählen kann, nur Ratschläge!»

«Nun kommen wir so langsam ans Ziel. Was ist mit ‹Möbel›?»

«Die sind nicht zählbar! Ein paar Möbel, ein Möbelstück!»

«Information?»

«Nicht zählbar! Some information, a piece of information!»

«Aber pass auf. Im Deutschen gibt es auch den Plural, ‹Informationen›! Wie sieht es mit Kuchen aus?»

«Zählbar! Ein Kuchen, zwei Kuchen, drei Kuchen!»

«Bist du sicher?»

«Selbstverständlich! Dieses zählbar/nicht zählbar ist ein … Sekunde mal …»

«Ja?»

«Ich kann Kuchen zählen, oder nicht?»

«Auf jeden Fall.»

«Aber ich kann auch sagen ‹etwas Kuchen› oder ‹ein Stück Kuchen›.»

"Correct."

"So?"

"So what?"

"Which is it? Countable or uncountable?"

"Both!"

"Both? How can it be both?"

"It depends on how you consider the cake."

"Well, my mum's cakes are the best in the world!"

"In that example, you are thinking of the many different cakes that your mother bakes."

"I certainly was. Her fruit cake is the best."

"Okay. Now which is sweeter, cake or bread?"

"Cake!"

"Sure?"

"Positive!"

"Can you give me a full sentence?"

"Cake is sweeter than bread. Bread is not as sweet as cake."

"Very good. When you were considering this, were you thinking of your mum's cakes?"

"No, just cake in general, just cake cake."

"Cake cake. I must remember that one. A bit like milk is milk."

"You know what I mean!"

"I'm pretty sure I do. You were thinking of uncountable cake!"

"I was?"

"Cake in general, cake cake."

"Right. I said that, didn't I?"

«Richtig.»

«Und?»

«Und was?»

«Was ist richtig? Zählbar oder nicht zählbar?»

«Beides!»

«Beides? Wie das denn?»

«Das kommt darauf an, wie du Kuchen betrachtest.»

«Nun, die Kuchen meiner Mutter sind die besten der Welt!»

«Bei diesem Beispiel denkst du an die vielen unterschiedlichen Kuchen, die deine Mutter bäckt.»

«Auf jeden Fall. Ihr Obstkuchen ist der beste.»

«Alles klar. Was ist süßer? Kuchen oder Brot?»

«Kuchen!»

«Sicher?»

«Ja, natürlich!»

«Kannst du einen ganzen Satz bilden?»

«Kuchen ist süßer also Brot. Brot ist nicht so süß wie Kuchen.»

«Sehr gut. Hast du hier an die Kuchen deiner Mutter gedacht?»

«Nein, nur Kuchen ganz allgemein. Kuchen Kuchen.»

«Kuchen Kuchen. Das muss ich mir merken. Das ist so ähnlich wie Milch ist Milch.»

«Du weißt schon, was ich meine.»

«Da bin ich mir ziemlich sicher. Du hast an nicht zählbaren Kuchen gedacht.»

«Habe ich?»

«Kuchen allgemein. Kuchen Kuchen.»

«Stimmt. Das habe ich gesagt, nicht wahr?»

"You certainly did. You also said 'cake is sweeter than bread'."

"That's right, isn't it?"

"Yes. But it's interesting that you said 'cake', rather than, 'a cake'."

"Excuse me, oh great one, but I don't find that particularly interesting."

"It is a fundamental difference between countable and uncountable nouns. An amazingly common error made by foreign learners. Almost all countable nouns take the indefinite article 'a' or 'an' when referred to in the singular."

"And the uncountable ones don't ! We don't say 'an advice' or 'a furniture', do we?"

"Indeed we don't. Can you see the kinds of problems that our foreign friends have with English?"

"I can indeed. Can I produce a quick table so that I don't forget countable and uncountable nouns?"

"Be my guest."

«Ja, stimmt. Du hast auch ‹Kuchen ist süßer als Brot› gesagt.»

«Das ist richtig. Stimmt das nicht?»

«Doch. Aber es ist interessant, dass du ‹Kuchen› gesagt hast und nicht ‹ein Kuchen›.»

«Entschuldigung, mein Meister. Aber das finde ich nicht besonders interessant.»

«Es gibt einen grundlegenden Unterschied zwischen zählbaren und nicht zählbaren Substantiven. Und das führt zu einem Fehler, den viele ausländische Schüler machen. Bei fast allen zählbaren Substantiven nimmt man den unbestimmten Artikel ‹a› oder ‹an›, wenn man sich auf die Singularform bezieht.»

«Und bei den nicht zählbaren nicht! Wir sagen nicht ‹an advice› oder ‹a furniture›, oder?»

«In der Tat. Kannst du die Probleme sehen, mit denen sich unsere ausländischen Freunde herumschlagen müssen?»

«Klar, kann ich. Kann ich schnell eine Tabelle machen, so dass ich die zählbaren und nicht zählbaren Substantive nicht vergesse?»

«Bitte schön!»

"Like it?"

"It's great, Barry."

"Thank you, oh great teacher. I am very impressed with the clarity with which you explained the differences ..."

"I can feel a 'but' coming."

"Can you remember the beginning of the lesson?"

"I can. I offered you a cup of tea."

"Cups are countable, tea is uncountable!"

"Correct."

	ZÄHLBARE SUBSTANTIVE	NICHT ZÄHLBARE SUBSTANTIVE
Kannst du sie zählen?	Ja: twenty-nine books, seven balls, two wheels ...	Nein: furniture, advice, gold, information
Wie kannst du sie unterscheiden?	‹a› oder ‹an› kann vor dem Substantiv stehen	Vor dem Substantiv kann nicht ‹a› oder ‹an› stehen.
Frageformen	How many cigarettes have you smoked?	How much time have you got for me?
Artikel	Ja: a dog, an ironing board, a cabbage	Nein: some rain, some love, some tea, some money
Pluralform	Ja (meistens)	Nein
Häufige Fehler*	Das Vergessen von Artikeln: My sister is [a] doctor. I've got [a] cold. Meine Schwester ist Ärztin. Ich habe Schnupfen.	Gebrauch falscher Pluralformen: Let me give you some [advice]s. Hinzufügung von Artikeln: She gave me an [some] information.

«Gefällt sie dir?»

«Sie sieht gut aus, Barry!»

«Danke dir, großer Meister. Ich bin von der Klarheit, mit der du mir den Unterschied erklärt hast, sehr beeindruckt.»

«Das hört sich so an, als ob da noch ein ‹aber› kommt.»

«Kannst du dich an den Anfang der Unterrichtsstunde erinnern?»

«Kann ich, ja. Ich habe dir eine Tasse Tee angeboten.»

«Tassen sind zählbar, Tee ist nicht zählbar!»

«Richtig.»

* korrekte Form in [...]

"You then offered me some milk."

"I did. I said, 'Would you like some milk?'."

"And I replied, 'Just a drop'. Milk is uncountable, drops are countable!"

"Right again."

"But then you offered me some sugar."

"I just said, 'Sugar?'."

"Do you remember my reply?"

"You said, 'three please'."

"Exactly! That was wrong! Sugar is uncountable!"

"Don't forget to have more faith in your own language. What do you mean, 'wrong'?"

"I should have said, 'three *spoonfuls* of sugar, please'. Shouldn't I?"

"Not at all. That was an example of ellipsis."

"Is that when the moon goes behind the sun?"

"Er, no, the sun is one hundred and fifty million kilometres away, I don't think the moon goes behind the sun very often. What you are thinking about is an *eclipse*."

"Total eclipse of the heart."

"Er, well, can we get back on with the lesson?"

"Sorry, I love Bonnie Tyler, me."

"Anyway, ellipsis is a linguistic term when a speaker or, less commonly, a writer drops words which they believe will be known to the listener or reader."

«Dann hast du mir Milch angeboten.»

«In der Tat. Ich habe ‹Möchtest du etwas Milch?› gesagt.»

«Und ich habe geantwortet: ‹Nur einen Tropfen.› Milch ist nicht zählbar, Tropfen sind es schon!»

«Stimmt auch.»

«Aber dann hast du mir Zucker angeboten.»

«Ich habe nur ‹Zucker?› gefragt.»

«Erinnerst du dich an meine Antwort?»

«Du sagtest: ‹Drei bitte.›»

«Genau! Das war falsch! Zucker ist nicht zählbar!»

«Denk dran, ein bisschen mehr Vertrauen in deine Sprachkenntnisse zu haben. Was meinst du mit ‹falsch›?»

«Ich hätte ‹drei Löffel Zucker, bitte› sagen sollen, oder nicht?»

«Ganz und gar nicht. Das war eine Ellipse.»

«Wenn der Mond hinter der Sonne verschwindet?»

«Hm, nein. Die Sonne ist einhundertfünfzig Millionen Kilometer entfernt. Ich kann mir kaum vorstellen, dass sich der Mond hinter der Sonne versteckt. Du hast an eine Eklipse gedacht.»

«Total eclipse of the heart.»

«Hm. Können wir jetzt mit dem Unterricht fortfahren?»

«Entschuldigung. Ich mag Bonnie Tyler einfach.»

«Egal. Ellipse ist ein linguistischer Ausdruck dafür, dass ein Redner, und seltener auch ein Autor, Wörter weglässt, von denen er glaubt, dass sie der Zuhörer beziehungsweise Leser gedanklich ergänzt.»

"Sorry, I'm a bit slow. Could you …?"

"Sure. You said, 'three please'. It was clear to me that you were referring to three *spoonfuls* of sugar, not three bucketfuls."

"I get you. But this 'ellipsis' is not very common, is it?"

"Not common? We use it all the time! Fancy a pint after class?"

"Yeah!"

"Did you notice my ellipsis?"

"Er, yes! You should have said, '*Do you* fancy a pint after class?'."

"I don't think I *should* have said 'Do you …'. You clearly understood what I wanted to say. Seen any good films recently?"

"You mean, *Have you* seen any good films recently?"

«Entschuldigung, bin ein wenig langsam. Könntest du …?»

«Klar doch. Du hast auf meine Frage nach Zucker ‹drei, bitte› geantwortet. Für mich war klar, dass du drei Löffel gemeint hast und nicht drei Eimer.»

«Verstehe. Aber Ellipsen sind nicht gerade häufig, oder?»

«Nicht häufig? Wir verwenden sie ständig! Nachher Lust auf ein Bier?»

«Ja!»

«Ist dir die Ellipse aufgefallen?»

«Hm, ja! Du hättest ‹Hast du im Anschluss an die Stunde Lust auf ein Bier?› sagen sollen.»

«Ja, aber das war nicht nötig. Du hast genau verstanden, was ich gemeint habe. Kürzlich ein paar gute Filme gesehen?»

«Du meinst ‹Hast du kürzlich ein paar gute Filme gesehen?›»

"You knew exactly what I meant. Ellipsis is incredibly common. Listen out for it!"

"Okay. Back to countable and uncountable. I have a final question."

"I'm waiting."

"What's that on top of your head?"

"Er, dandruff?"

"No, those bits of stuff growing out of your head."

"Hmm, I think you should practise your simple explanations. Can I presume you were referring to my hair?"

"You can. Now, how *many* hairs have got on your head?"

"I've never counted but I believe around one hundred thousand."

"One hundred thousand *countable* hairs?"

"Yes."

"So when I asked you initially, why did you use the form 'hair' in the singular form?"

"Good question. Sometimes students say, 'you have beautiful hairs' and you should correct them. The reason we use the singular form is simply because we are referring to a head of hair, hair being considered, like cake, as an uncountable noun."

"Thought so."

"So why are you smiling?"

"Well, at the moment you have hair …"

"What are you implying? I have a fine head of hair. I just like to keep it short."

«Du hast genau verstanden, was ich gemeint habe. Ellipsen sind unglaublich häufig. Hör einfach genau hin!»

«Okay. Zurück zu zählbar und nicht zählbar. Ich habe noch eine letzte Frage.»

«Schieß los.»

«Was hast du auf dem Kopf?»

«Schuppen?»

«Ne, die Dinger die dir da aus dem Kopf wachsen.»

«Hm. Ich glaube, du solltest deine einfachen Erklärungen noch ein bisschen üben. Kann ich davon ausgehen, dass du mein Haar gemeint hast?»

«Kannst du. Wie viele Haare hast du auf deinem Kopf?»

«Die habe ich nie gezählt. Aber ich glaube, es sind ungefähr hunderttausend.»

«Hunderttausend zählbare Haare?»

«Ja.»

«Warum hast du, als ich dich das erste Mal gefragt habe, ‹Haar› im Singular verwendet?»

«Gute Frage. Manchmal sagen die Schüler: ‹You have beautiful hairs›, dann solltest du sie korrigieren. Der Grund, warum wir die Singularform verwenden, ist schlicht und einfach der, dass wir uns auf einen Kopf voller Haar beziehen. Haar wird so wie Kuchen verwendet, als nicht zählbares Substantiv.»

«Das habe ich mir gedacht.»

«Warum grinst du dann so?»

«Nun, im Moment hast du ja Haar ...»

«Was willst du damit sagen? Ich habe volles Haar. Ich halte es nur ganz kurz.»

"Well, you are going a little thin on top. A head of fine hair but quite a few less than last week I think."

"That is outrageous!"

"My question is, how many hairs do you have to lose before we should stop saying 'I like your hair', and start saying 'I like your hairs'?"

"I am not going thin on top, Barry Buggins! I have a fine head of hair and don't you forget that!"

«Ein bisschen schütterer wirst du ja. Schönes Haar, wirklich, aber doch deutlich lichter als letzte Woche, scheint mir.»

«Das ist ungeheuerlich!»

«Meine Frage ist, wie viele Haare musst du noch verlieren, bevor wir aufhören müssen zu sagen: ‹Ich mag dein Haar›, und anfangen müssen zu sagen: ‹Ich mag deine Haare›?»

«Meine Haarpracht wird nicht schütterer, Barry Buggins. Ich habe eine schöne Haarpracht. Vergiss das ja nicht!»

 JUST FOR...

"Hi, Barry. It's our last session together."

"It is. Are you going to miss me?"

"I think there is a chance that my eyes might remain dry when we part."

"I think that was an insult, but I'll let it go. So, what are we going to look at today?"

"Well, as you're planning to work in Germany I think it makes sense that we have a look at typical errors that affect Germans."

"Don't mention the war!"

"Yes, that would be inappropriate, but I was thinking more of errors that Germans make rather than all the faux pas that you could make."

"I don't even know what a faux pas is so it's pretty unlikely I'll make one."

Nur für Deutsche

«Hallo, Barry. Heute haben wir unsere letzte Stunde.»

«Ja. Wirst du mich vermissen?»

«Es kann durchaus sein, dass meine Augen trocken bleiben, wenn wir Abschied nehmen.»

«Wenn das keine Beleidigung war. Aber ich sag mal nichts. Was werden wir uns heute anschauen?»

«Da du planst, in Deutschland zu arbeiten, macht es durchaus Sinn, uns ein paar Fehler anzusehen, die vorrangig Deutsche betreffen.»

«Erwähne den Krieg nicht!»

«Ja, das wäre absolut unpassend. Aber eigentlich habe ich eher an Fehler gedacht, die Deutsche machen, als an all die Fauxpas, die dir unterlaufen könnten.»

«Ich weiß nicht einmal, was ein Fauxpas ist. Also eher unwahrscheinlich, dass mir ein solcher unterläuft.»

"Well, I guess your future students will be the judges of that. So, let's start off with some of the most common mistakes that Germans do …"

"Okay, I'm waiting …"

"Some of the most common mistakes that Germans do …"

"I heard you the first time. I'm waiting for you to … wait a minute. We don't do mistakes, we make them!"

"Glad you got there in the end. So we *make mistakes*, what about homework? Have you made your homework?"

"What homework? Wait a minute, we don't make homework, we *do home- work*!"

"Well, some people do. What about … house- work?"

"No, I don't do that. Oh sorry; we *do house- work*!"

"Correct. Decisions?"

"We *make decisions*!"

"Suggestions?"

"We *make suggestions*!"

"As a native speaker it's no surprise that you're getting these right. You've grown up with them."

"But it will be harder for my lovely students to *make progress*!"

"Very true. Okay next one that not only Germans but plenty of native speakers have a

«Nun, ich denke, deine zukünftigen Schüler werden sich darüber ein Urteil bilden. Lass uns jetzt mit einigen der Englischfehler beginnen, die Deutsche am häufigsten tun.»

«Okay. Ich warte …»

«Einige der häufigsten Fehler, die Deutsche immer wieder tun …»

«Ich habe dich schon beim ersten Mal verstanden. Ich warte darauf … Moment mal, man sagt nicht Fehler tun, sondern Fehler machen!»

«Freut mich, dass du noch draufgekommen bist. Wir machen also Fehler. Was ist mit Hausaufgaben? Hast du deine Hausaufgaben getan?»

«Welche Hausaufgaben? Wart mal kurz. Im Englischen sagt man nicht ‹make homework› sondern ‹do homework›.»

«Nun, manche Leute durchaus schon. Wie steht es mit … Hausarbeit?»

«Schlecht. Ups, Entschuldigung – wir machen die Hausarbeit!»

«Richtig. Entscheidungen?»

«Wir treffen Entscheidungen!»

«Vorschläge?»

«Wir machen Vorschläge!»

«Als Muttersprachler machst du hier natürlich alles richtig. Du bist mit all dem aufgewachsen.»

«Aber für meine lieben Schüler wird es schwieriger sein, Fortschritte zu machen!»

«Stimmt genau. Nun zum nächsten. Damit haben nicht nur Deutsche, die Englisch lernen, sondern auch

problem with as well. Let's take a look out the window. What can you see?"

"There's a bunch of students sitting on a bench."

"And what are they doing?"

"Staring at their mobiles!"

"Are they here, staring at their mobiles?"

"Your questions are pretty weird sometimes."

"Just answer the question please, Barry."

"No, they're not here. They're over there, staring at their ... Oh wow, that's pretty weird."

"What is?"

"All those 'there's'."

"Can you talk me through 'all those there's'?"

"I'll give it a shot. The first one is 'they're' a contraction of 'they are' as we've already talked about the bunch of students."

"Going well so far."

"The second one is 'there', showing position, not here, but there."

"Good, can you make it three out of three?"

"And the third one is 'their' – as the mobiles belong to them, the students!"

"Brilliant work! 'Their' is a possessive pronoun. I think you could be the next Professor of Linguistics at Cambridge University!"

"Nah, not me. I'm going to work in Germany! Which reminds me, do Germans have the same problem with 'the there's'?"

"Some of them do, particularly if they pick up

ganz viele englische Muttersprachler ein Problem. Schauen wir mal aus dem Fenster. Was siehst du?»

«Eine Gruppe Schüler, die auf einer Bank sitzt.»

«Und was machen die da?»

«Die starren auf ihre Handys.»

«Sind sie hier und starren auf ihre Handys?»

«Deine Fragen sind manchmal sehr komisch.»

«Beantworte einfach nur die Frage, Barry.»

«Nein, sie sind nicht hier. Sie sind dort drüben und starren auf ihre ... Auweia, das wird doch ziemlich komisch.»

«Was denn?»

«Alle diese ‹there's› im Englischen.»

«Kannst du mir die nicht erklären?»

«Ich probier's mal. Das erste ‹they're› ist die Kurzform von ‹they are›, so wie im Satz mit der Gruppe Studenten, von der wir gesprochen haben.»

«Geht doch schon ganz gut.»

«Das zweite ist ‹there›, also ein lokaler Bezug, nicht hier, sondern eben dort.»

«Gut und das dritte?»

«Das dritte ist ‹their› – die Handys gehören ihnen, also den Schülern!»

«Hervorragend, ein Possessivpronomen also! Ich denke, du könntest dich zu einem Linguistikprofessor an der Uni Cambridge mausern!»

«Oh ne, das ist nichts für mich. Ich werde in Deutschland arbeiten. Wie sieht das denn mit den Deutschen aus. Haben die dieselben Probleme mit den ‹there's›?»

«Einige von ihnen schon, vor allem diejenigen, die

most of their English by listening to music. The students who read a lot are less likely to make the error as they see the 'there's' written down."

"That makes sense. Oh, that's another one for my 'make and do' list!"

"So, Barry, what kind of music do you like hearing?"

"For some reason that sounds pretty strange to me."

"So how would you correct the sentence?"

"What kind of music do you like listening to?"

"So I can't hear music …"

"Well, you can …"

"But?"

"I'm not sure."

"Don't worry, most native speakers can't explain it either but your German students will have studied it at school but may well have forgotten it."

"Why do German students learn English grammar but we don't?"

"Well, not knowing the difference between the two hasn't damaged your life so far, has it?"

"True. But please explain the difference between 'listen to' and 'hear'."

"Last night I listened to someone scream outside my flat."

"That sounds very weird. It sounds like you sat in a comfortable chair and actively listened

Englisch überwiegend durch Musikhören lernen. Schüler, die viel lesen, machen diesen Fehler seltener, da sie sehen, wie diese ‹there's› geschrieben werden.»

«Das macht Sinn. Ich nehme das auch gleich in meine Make-do-Liste auf!»

«Welche Art von Musik hörst du denn gerne, Barry?»

«‹Hearing›? Irgendwie klingt das in meinen Ohren komisch.»

«Was wäre denn richtig?»

«Hier würde ich ‹listening› nehmen.»

«Man kann hier also nicht ‹hear music› nehmen.»

«Das kann man schon …»

«Aber?»

«Ich bin mir nicht ganz sicher …»

«Mach dir nichts draus. Die meisten englischen Muttersprachler können das auch nicht erklären. Aber deine deutschen Schüler werden das in der Schule gelernt, aber womöglich wieder vergessen haben.»

«Warum lernen deutsche Schüler englische Grammatik, wir aber nicht?»

«Nun, dass du den Unterschied zwischen beiden nicht erklären kannst, hat dir bisher auch nicht geschadet, oder?»

«Stimmt wohl. Aber kannst du mir trotzdem den Unterschied zwischen ‹zuhören› und ‹hören› erklären?»

«Gestern Nacht habe ich jemandem zugehört (to listen), der vor meiner Wohnung geschrien hat.»

«Das klingt sehr komisch. Es klingt, als ob du in einem bequemen Sessel gesessen und jemandem ein, zwei Stun-

to someone scream for an hour or two – which I hope was not the case."

"Correct. And I like your use of the word 'actively'. You can hear things you don't want to hear, any sound that enters your ears but if you listen to something, you do so actively."

"Wow, I'd never thought about the difference."

"It's quite similar to 'see', 'look' and 'watch'."

"I see loads of things, whether I want to or not. I can look at something if I want to but probably just for a short time but if I watch something I do it actively probably for some time. Examples: Sometimes I see a beautiful woman in the park. I look at my phone every ten minutes. In the zoo I like watching the monkeys."

"You know, Barry, I think one day you might be able to teach English."

den aufmerksam beim Schreien zugehört hättest – und ich hoffe wirklich, dass dem so nicht war.»

«Richtig. Und mir gefällt besonders gut, dass du das Wort ‹aufmerksam› benutzt hast. Du kannst auch Dinge hören (to hear), die du nicht hören willst, irgendwelche Laute, die an dein Ohr dringen. Aber wenn du ‹zuhören› (to listen) benutzt, dann tust du das aufmerksam.»

«Wow, ich wäre nie auf diesen Unterschied gekommen.»

«Das ist so ähnlich wie mit ‹sehen› (to see), ‹(an-)schauen› (to look) und ‹zuschauen› (to watch).»

«Ich sehe viele Dinge, ob ich will oder nicht. Ich kann etwas anschauen, wenn ich möchte, aber womöglich nur für kurze Zeit. Aber wenn ich etwas oder jemandem zuschaue, dann tue ich das aufmerksam und wahrscheinlich über einen längeren Zeitraum hinweg. Ich nenne einmal Beispiele. Manchmal sehe ich eine schöne Frau im Park. Ich schaue alle zehn Minuten auf mein Handy. Im Tierpark schaue ich gern den Affen zu.»

«Weißt du was, Barry? Eines Tages kannst du wahrscheinlich doch Englisch unterrichten.»

"Wow, I don't think I've ever heard such sweet words."

"But there's still plenty to look at."

"I'm sure there is."

"So let's move on with some more things that Germans have problems with. Do you like my tie?"

"I can understand the problems Germans might have with your tie. Ha ha."

"Very funny, Barry. I bought this tie for three years."

"What? You can't use 'for' with simple past! You can't say that!"

"Well, I just did. I bought this tie for three years."

"Wait a minute. I saw you pointing over your shoulder and I know what that means; it means in the past! You bought that tie three years ago!"

"Very good. In German they say 'vor drei Jahren' so you can understand how they make the mistake."

"I get it."

"I once had a German student who gave me her business card and told me she would write her new handy number on the backside."

"I know that Germans call a mobile phone a 'handy' but on whose backside did she want to write the number? It sounds a bit kinky to me."

"She wanted to write it on the backside of her business card."

«Wow, solche netten Worte hab ich wohl noch nie gehört.»

«Aber wir haben noch einiges vor uns.»

«Dessen bin ich mir sicher.»

«Lass uns also noch ein paar weitere Dinge anschauen, mit denen Deutsche Probleme haben. Was hältst du von meiner Krawatte?»

«Ich sehe das Problem, das Deutsche mit deiner Krawatte haben. Haha.»

«Sehr witzig, Barry. Ich habe diese Krawatte vor drei Jahren gekauft.»

«Was? ‹For three years› und die Vergangenheit benutzen? Das kannst du nicht machen!»

«Kann ich wohl. I bought this tie for three years.»

«Wart mal kurz. Ich habe gesehen, wie du über deine Schulter gezeigt hast, und das bedeutet, dass etwas in der Vergangenheit liegt! Du hast die Krawatte vor drei Jahren gekauft!»

«Sehr gut. Auf Deutsch sagt man ‹vor drei Jahren›. Verstehst du daher, warum deutsche Schüler diesen Fehler machen?»

«Verstehe.»

«Ich hatte einmal eine deutsche Schülerin, die mir ihre Visitenkarte gab und sagte, sie würde ihre neue Handynummer auf den Hintern schreiben.»˜

«Ich weiß, dass Deutsche ein Mobiltelefon ‹Handy› nennen. Aber auf wessen Hintern wollte sie die Nummer schreiben? Das hört sich für mich doch etwas obszön an.»

«Sie wollte die Nummer auf den Hintern ihrer Visitenkarte schreiben.»

"Ah, you mean on the back!"

"Exactly."

"And she said backside! Ha ha ha. That's hilarious!"

"Your students won't appreciate you laughing at them. Laugh with them, but not at them."

"Okay, boss. Have you got any more funny ones?"

"Well, you'll find out sooner or later, do you know the German word for 'journey'?"

"Not yet."

"The word is 'Fahrt'."

"Fart? As in, 'pass wind'?"

"Yes, though the German Fahrt is spelt F-a-h-r-t."

"But pronounced 'fart'."

"Yes."

"The Fahrt was long!"

"Very amusing."

"I enjoyed the Fahrt but I'm not sure the people around me did."

"Okay, Barry, I think that's enough Fahrt jokes. Another word that Germans regularly misuse is the word 'become'."

"I'm going to become the best teacher Germany has ever seen!"

"Er, yes. But in German the word 'bekommen' means 'to get'. The classic joke is that a German goes into a restaurant and says, 'I want to become a steak'. In fact I've noticed that

«Ach, du meinst die Rückseite?»

«Genau.»

«Aber sie hat ‹Hintern› gesagt! Haha, ich brech gleich zusammen vor Lachen!»

«Deine Schüler werden es sicher nicht mögen, wenn du sie auslachst. Lach lieber mit ihnen anstatt über sie.»

«Alles klar, Chef. Hast du noch ein paar lustige Beispiele auf Lager?»

«Du wirst das früher oder später selbst herausfinden. Kennst du das deutsche Wort für ‹journey›?»

«Noch nicht.»

«Es heißt ‹Fahrt›.»

«Furz? Wie in ‹einen fahren lassen›?»

«Stimmt. Aber das deutsche Fahrt wird F-a-h-r-t geschrieben.»

«Aber gleich ausgesprochen?»

«Ja!»

«Die Fahrt war lang!»

«Sehr lustig.»

«Ich habe die Fahrt genossen, bin mir aber nicht sicher, ob die Leute um mich herum das Gleiche sagen würden.»

«Gut, Barry. Ich denke das sind genug Fahrt-Witze. Ein weiteres Wort, das Deutsche oft in falschem Zusammenhang verwenden, ist ‹become›.»

«Ich werde der beste Lehrer, den Deutschland je gesehen hat!»

«Hm, na ja. Aber das deutsche Wort ‹bekommen› heißt auf Englisch ‹to get›. Kennst du den klassischen Witz über einen Deutschen, der in ein Restaurant geht und sagt: ‹Ich möchte ein Steak werden.›? Es sieht so

Germans now avoid using the verb 'become' in English. They'll say things like, 'In the future I'd like to be a really good teacher', simply to avoid the verb 'become' as they think they might get it wrong."

"I'll try to remember that."

"You may well hear some students say they are interested in old timers."

"Why would they be interested in old men?"

"They aren't. In German the term for a vintage car is an 'old timer'."

"So, I had a long Fahrt with an old timer …"

"Thank you, Barry. Let's do a few more. You may hear your students say, 'I work by T-Mobile'."

"I work for T-mobile! Unless they mean 'next to' T-Mobile."

"No, I think you were right the first time. And what if a German says, 'What time do you stand up in the morning?'."

"That sounds like a very intimate question."

"Not at all. It's a translation of the German word 'aufstehen' which means 'to get up'."

"Get up, stand up, stand up for your rights! I love Bob Marley, me. Perhaps he taught English in Germany as well."

"Not to the best of my knowledge. You'll

aus, als ob Deutsche im Englischen mehr und mehr versuchen, das Verb ‹become› zu umgehen. Sie sagen dann zum Beispiel: ‹Ich möchte später einmal ein richtig guter Lehrer sein.› Sie wollen einfach das Verb ‹become› vermeiden, um ja nichts falsch zu machen.»

«Ich versuche, das zu behalten.»

«Vielleicht bekommst du auch einmal Schüler, die sagen, sie seien an alten Männern interessiert.»

«Warum sollten sie sich für alte Männer interessieren?»

«Tun sie nicht. Der deutsche Begriff für ‹vintage car› ist ‹Oldtimer›.»

«Nun, ich hatte eine lange Fahrt mit einem alten Mann …»

«Danke dir, Barry. Lass uns noch ein paar durchnehmen. Vielleicht hörst du deine Schüler einmal ‹I work by T-Mobile› sagen.»

«‹I work for T-Mobile!›. Außer sie meinen tatsächlich ‹next to›, also neben T-Mobile.»

«Nein, ich denke, dein erster Vorschlag war richtig. Und was meint ein Deutscher mit ‹What time do you stand up in the morning?›»

«Das klingt nach einer ziemlich vertraulichen Frage.»

«Ganz und gar nicht. Das ist die direkte Übersetzung des deutschen Wortes ‹aufstehen›, also eigentlich ‹to get up›.»

«Get up, stand up, stand up for your rights! Der gute Bob Marley. Vielleicht hat auch er in Deutschland Englisch unterrichtet.»

«Soviel ich weiß, nicht. Wahrscheinlich hast du

probably have students who say 'I live in the near of Mannheim'."

"In the near of Mannheim? I presume they mean 'I live near Mannheim' but why the extra bits?"

"It's a translation error. 'Ich wohne in der Nähe von Mannheim.' You can see how such mistakes are made."

"Well, I can, but it's hard to believe that Germans make basic errors like this. I thought they were pretty smart people."

"I think you'll find they *are* very smart people and many new English teachers get eaten for breakfast by German students who know a lot more about English than their English teachers."

"Point taken. Humble pie eaten."

"A little humility will go a long way. I'm sure you'll find that ninety-nine per cent of Germans are lovely people who work hard, play hard and are very keen to communicate whatever their level of English."

"I get it. And thanks for guiding me through so much English grammar. I feel 'fixed' now and ready for Germany. What's the German word for 'ready'?"

"Fertig."

auch Schüler, die ‹ I live in the near of Mannheim › sagen. »

« In the near of Mannheim? Ich denke, die meinen ‹ I live near Mannheim ›. Aber warum das ‹ the ›? »

« Das ist ein Übersetzungsfehler. ‹ Ich wohne in der Nähe von Mannheim. › Da kannst du sehen, wie solche Fehler entstehen. »

« Ja, das kann ich. Aber es ist kaum zu glauben, dass Deutsche so grundlegende Fehler wie diese machen sollen. Ich dachte, sie wären ziemlich klug. »

« Du wirst sehen, viele sind sehr klug. Und viele angehende Englischlehrer werden von ihren deutschen Schülern, die über Englisch viel mehr als ihre Englischlehrer wissen, zum Frühstück verspeist. »

« Kapiert! Ich krieche zu Kreuze. »

« Ein wenig Demut schadet nichts. Du wirst sicher schnell merken, dass neunundneunzig Prozent der Deutschen liebenswerte Menschen sind, die hart arbeiten, zu feiern wissen und sehr daran interessiert sind, mit dir zu reden, egal auf welchem Sprachniveau sie sich befinden. »

« Kapiert. Und vielen Dank, dass du mich durch so viel englische Grammatik gelotst hast. Ich fühle mich nun ganz gut gerüstet. Was sagt man auf Deutsch für ‹ ready ›? »

« ‹ Bereit › oder ‹ fertig ›. »

*Two months later in a language school at an
undisclosed location in Germany*

"Hallo ! Ich bin Barry Buggins. Ich komme von
England. The Fahrt was lang. Ich bin fix und fertig !"

« Hallo ! Ich bin Barry Buggins. Ich komme von England. The Fahrt was lang. Ich bin fix und fertig ! »

Sprache verbindet

dtv

نصوص عربية أَوَّلِيَة

Erste arabische Lesestücke

Herausgegeben von Claudia Ott

dtv

zhōng wén yuè dù rù mén
中 文 阅 读 入 门

Erste chinesische
Lesestücke

dtv

Lektura dla
początkujących

Erste polnische
Lesestücke

dtv

Книга
для первого
чтения

Erste russische
Lesestücke

Die fabelhafte Welt der Märchen in kultureller und sprachlicher Vielfalt entdecken

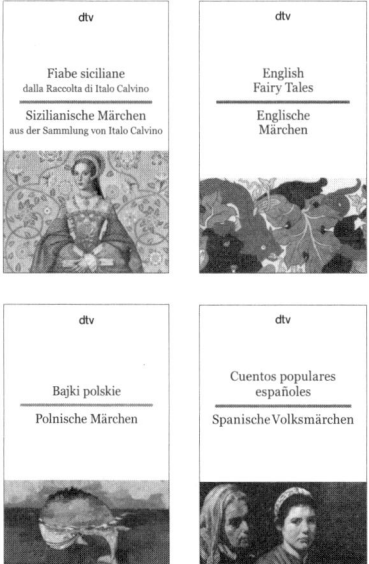

Spielerisch leicht lesen und lernen

ALLE LIEFERBAREN TITEL, INFORMATIONEN UND SPECIALS
FINDEN SIE ONLINE

www.dtv.de